C0-BXA-871

Best Technology Practices in Higher Education

Best Technology Practices in Higher Education

Edited by
Les Lloyd

Information Today, Inc.
Medford, New Jersey

First printing, 2005

Best Technology Practices in Higher Education

Library of Congress Cataloging-in-Publication Data

Best technology practices in higher education / edited by Les Lloyd.
p. cm.
Includes bibliographical references.
ISBN 1-57387-208-3 (pbk.)
1. Education, Higher--Computer-assisted instruction. 2. Education, Higher--Effect of technological innovations on. 3. Information technology. 4. Educational technology. I. Lloyd, Les.
LB2395.7.B48 2004
378.1'734--dc22
2004009778

Publisher: Thomas H. Hogan, Sr.
Editor-in-Chief: John B. Bryans
Managing Editors: Deborah R. Poulson, Amy M. Holmes
Graphics Department Director: M. Heide Dengler
Copy Editor: Pat Hadley-Miller
Book Designer: Kara Mia Jalkowski
Cover Designer: Michele Quinn
Indexer: Sharon Hughes

For a complete catalog, contact:
Information Today, Inc.
143 Old Marlton Pike, Medford, NJ 08055 • 609/654-6266
email: custserv@infotoday.com • Web site: www.infotoday.com

Contents

Figures

Tables

Dedication

This book is dedicated to Dr. Rita Bornstein, former President of Rollins College, whose leadership inspired us. Dr. Bornstein came to Rollins in 1990 when it was known as a nice, small, Florida school. During her 14-year tenure, she raised money, built buildings, added and strengthened programs and, most importantly, set out to make Rollins the number one college of choice for incoming students. Her legacy, aside from the transformation of the campus, is of a college on the move with 30 percent more students, a nine-fold increase in endowment, a national reputation, and the pride felt by students, faculty, and staff who see how far we've come and how much we can achieve together. It has been an honor to serve under her leadership.

Dedication

Foreword

Information technology has profoundly impacted colleges and universities. However, the remarkable benefits of rapid information transfer often seem offset by the rapid pace of technological advances. In this atmosphere, decision-making with regard to technology has major budget and operation implications.

Best Technology Practices in Higher Education, authored by national and international experts in the field, provides information on the most important technology issues in higher education. The result is a clear, practical guide that can be of great use to higher education administrators.

Les Lloyd, associate vice-president for Information Technology at Rollins College, deserves high praise for the conception, development, and coordination of the original symposium that served as the basis for this volume, and for his judicious editing of these proceedings. His efforts provide us with an admirable model of how higher education administrators, in the course of their specific professional responsibilities, can at the same time continue to serve as model teachers and scholars.

Anne B. Kerr, Ph.D.
President, Florida Southern College

Introduction

Many management courses use case studies as a means to teach the "right" and "wrong" way to handle specific situations. Given the same problem, though, six people could reasonably come up with different solutions that all worked as needed. So, although the "Best Practices" presented here are meant to showcase solutions, they are by no means the only way these problems could have been addressed. The authors and I did use as a guiding principle, though, that these projects could be easily replicated at many other schools, and that the costs of implementation wouldn't render any project financially unfeasible. Our definition of best practices is: proven solutions to common problems that are available to institutions for adoption regardless of the hardware or software used.

In planning to teach the course Management of Communication Technology in our Master's of Corporate Communication and Technology graduate program, it struck me that it was going to be very difficult to teach a course on what I do every day. How could I present the vast array of options and solutions to students with a wide range of technical skills and interests? Clearly, trying to condense 20-plus years of making decisions, right or wrong, into a semester-long course was going to be a real challenge.

So, we come back to case studies to demonstrate a specific set of variables that led to a problem, show the resources available to deal with the problem, and then let the reader work through solutions. One can never present all the possible permutations of problems that occur daily; what we can teach, though, is a method of problem solving that should yield positive results most of the time, which is the reason for putting together a volume like this.

You won't have the same set of problems illustrated here, but you may have similar ones. You may find a solution that can work for you, or an idea, or make the acquaintance of someone who can help you work through your own complicated set of variables. The topics included in this work are illustrative of the variety of issues that face the information technology industry in general, and IT on college campuses specifically. Some of the projects are major; others are modest. Hopefully, you'll discover at least one that solves a problem, suggests a useful new service, or sparks a winning idea.

It is not my intention to present a comprehensive set of best practices in this book—a volume like that might be impossible to create. However, there are other best practices that I thought would be worth mentioning, for those that are new to the field or looking for more examples. These include:

- **Information technology organization:** Much has been written in recent years about to whom the chief technology officer should report: the president, the chief academic officer, or the chief administrative officer. Depending on politics, this can be a major issue related to the funding and importance of IT in the organization, or it can be a nonissue. The key is that IT report to an influential person who can represent the technology needs of the institution to whoever makes the final budget and policy decisions. Whether this is a provost influencing a president or a president influencing a board of trustees is unimportant. This is the reason why there is no standard reporting structure for Chief Information Officers (CIOs).

- **Selecting administrative software:** Just about every college that hasn't converted its administrative software system to one of the market leaders will do so in the next few years. The advantages of having built-in Web functionality alone justify the cost of the project for most schools. Administrative software has followed the trend of library packages; 20 years ago there were many vendors and products. Today there are a few, and virtually every college, except some major research institutions, owns one of these packages. The fallout on the administrative software side has been similar, with SCT's Banner seemingly dominating the market and many smaller vendors falling by the wayside. Oracle's announcement of its intention to purchase PeopleSoft, SCT's only significant competitor at this time, demonstrates how fast the market situation can change. Most colleges have learned that they can't write software in-house that's flexible to meet changes, that can withstand the constant turnover of programmers, and that can compete functionally with these major market packages.

- **Internet portals:** Software that integrates multiple on-campus systems into a single sign-on or access-point

> combining e-mail, access to student records systems, and course delivery systems are a similar development point of the administrative software programs of 15 years ago. There are many sources of portals. Some are home-grown (State University at Buffalo, George Washington University), some are add-ons to administrative software packages (Campus Pipeline/Luminis, PeopleSoft), and some are provided by course management systems or bookstore vendors (Blackboard, Follett). My prediction is that the same thing will happen here as with library and administrative software: a couple of major vendors will dominate the field and most schools will ultimately purchase a commercial portal.

The book has been divided into four parts to help you navigate the material:

- Teaching: presents solutions that impact the teaching or distribution of courses
- Administrative: presents solutions geared to effective and efficient college operations and/or services
- Technical: showcases solutions that integrate various technologies or operations or provide for more effective technical administration
- Future projects: outlines projects that make sense to consider now but may not be feasible for several years

Each of these topic areas presents significant opportunities for colleges to distinguish themselves from others, to change the way we teach and how we run our operations. The cases discussed in the book illustrate how some schools have leveraged technology to provide better services or course delivery to their constituents. It is my hope that your school will benefit from the experiences presented in the pages that follow. Please send feedback to me at Les.Lloyd@Rollins.edu. And if you have a case study of your own you'd like to share, let me know—perhaps I will include it in a follow-up to *Best Technology Practices in Higher Education.*

Part 1

Best Practices in Teaching and Course Delivery

Aside from distance learning, one of the biggest topics in technology-enriched teaching is that of electronic portfolios. While there are many models, the basic premise is the same. Students maintain an electronic journal of their college experiences allowing and encouraging them to demonstrate a proficiency with the material they've learned and thoughtful reflection on the path they've chosen. A senior's portfolio should show how course selections influenced major choice and career path and how extracurricular activities added to that experience. Other versions of electronic portfolios provide for smaller projects based on a particular course, a study-abroad experience, or a career-related portfolio used for education and other specific majors.

Several chapters in Part 1 reflect on distance or online learning, including a project on lecture delivery online. The Associated Colleges of the South chapter on creating a course delivery system wrestles with interesting issues. Most schools have chosen a commercial package such as WebCT®, Blackboard®, or one of a handful of others. Many schools have been concerned with these vendors' pricing policies and/or their slow record of making changes to the software based on user feedback. Both companies provided very inexpensive sign-on fees several years ago and now that schools have adopted them as standards, prices have risen geometrically. While there are some provisions to continue "using the old version" of the software, there is no doubt that at some point everyone will have to pay the new fees. The ACS consortium is taking another view on the issue and writing an open source courseware system that other schools may share. This allows for customizing without the annual maintenance fees that make the commercial packages less attractive. But what does one do when faculty have chosen a package for the campus? Are faculty willing to redo their online classes to save money for the IT department? Can consortial software coders create market-compatible software, keep the pricing free or low cost and ensure that member schools won't be left without support in the future? We've seen this example before with administrative software packages, such as AIMS, where the vendor sold the source code to a group of schools to maintain.

One concern of online instructors is how to ensure that the person taking an exam is the person registered for the class. This is one of the topics addressed by Carole Hayes in Chapter 2.

Finally, one of the keys to ensuring that faculty can use all the new and changing technology is a regular program for faculty instruction that takes place at times convenient for their schedules. This is discussed in Chapter 5, by Mollie Gore of Charleston Southern University.

CHAPTER 1

Electronic Portfolios

Dr. Terry Corwin
Director of Instructional Technology
Valley City State University

Introduction

A member of the North Dakota University System, Valley City State University (VCSU) is a leader in the effective use of instructional technologies and offers baccalaureate degrees in education, business, and the liberal arts. With a student population of 1,100, VCSU is among the smallest public baccalaureates in the nation; however, there is nothing small about its ambitions.

In 1995 VCSU adopted an electronic portfolio initiative and in 1996 became the second four-year laptop institution in the nation, providing laptop computers to all of its faculty and students.

Its mission statement confirms the significance of learner-centered instruction, innovation, and instructional technology as hallmarks of VCSU's efforts to prepare individuals to serve in a changing world.

The bold initiatives VCSU has undertaken in the last ten years demonstrate its innovative spirit and willingness to adapt while remaining on the frontier of best practice. The integration of technology in teaching and learning through the laptop initiative and the digital portfolios represent just two innovations. VCSU has also created the nation's only Technology Education program that (a) meets new national standards in this field and (b) is available online. Over 70 percent of faculty have adopted online course software (Blackboard) as a tool for their classes. Each initiative was undertaken for the purpose of giving students a more flexible (customized) learning environment and expanding the possibilities of a learner-centered education. A student survey provides evidence of the university's student-centered environment. Results of the survey and more information concerning VCSU's student-centered experience can be found in a report on the VCSU Web site (Holleque, 1998 April).

Best Technology Practices Project

The Best Technology Practices project became visible on the campus in November 1995. It was designed to employ ability-based assessment as a tool in the curricula and enable students to complete an electronic portfolio on CD-ROM. VCSU secured a five-year Title III grant of $850,000 for the project. The grant funded equipment, personnel, and support for faculty training and stipends. It also enabled the portfolio process to become a campuswide initiative from its inception. Figure 1.1 provides an example of the VCSU senior portfolio. The portfolio presents a "best works" collection of student projects illustrating the student's competence in the eight University Abilities.

Figure 1.1 Portfolio

Table 1.1 Abilities and Skills

1. **Communications**
   - Written
   - Visual
   - Spoken
   - Performance
2. **Problem solving**
   - Gathering Information
   - Problem Recognition
   - Creative Thinking
   - Systems Analysis
   - Decision Making
3. **Collaboration**
   - Positive Interdependence
   - Leadership
4. **Technology**
   - Selects
   - Applies
5. **Effective Citizenship**
   - Provides Service to Others
   - Teaches Others
   - Change Agent Skills
6. **Aesthetic Engagement**
   - Receptivity
   - Visualization
7. **Global Perspectives**
   - Works with Diversity
   - Understands System Interrelationships
8. **Wellness**
   - Self Management
   - Self Worth

The 8 abilities and 22 skills endorsed by the institution are the fundamental underpinnings of the portfolio. The VCSU faculty authored the abilities and skills and the faculty senate adopted them. Table 1.1 displays the 8 abilities and the 22 skills that define the abilities. Nearly every academic course includes an ability-based project assignment. The senior portfolio provides documentation of the student's achievement of the abilities.

The diffusion of the portfolio process began with a 10-member faculty learning team, representative of the academic divisions. The team members discussed the portfolio process and made decisions concerning the purpose, audience, and expectations of the senior portfolio. Among the articles read and reviewed by the team were *Linking Assessment with Reform: Technologies that Support Conversations about Student Work* (Sheingold and Frederiksen, 1995), *Portfolios Across the Curriculum and Beyond* (Cole, Ryan, and Kick, 1995), and *Portfolio Assessment: Some Questions, Some Answers, Some Recommendations* (Gillespie, Ford, Gillespie, and Leavell, 1996). The Learning Team members also received training in the hardware and software needed to create multimedia projects. The second year of the implementation process included one-on-one mentoring for 10 more faculty each semester. The process continued until, by the end of the fourth year, 85 percent of the faculty had been mentored. In the fifth year (1999), a priority was placed on mentoring new faculty. In addition, faculty stipends were provided

Table 1.2 Business Administration Ability Map

Division Outcome	Ability	Skill	Targeted Levels / Classes				
			Level 1				
To convey thoughts, ideas, data, information and messages effectively	Communication	Written			BVED 340	MGMT 480	
		Spoken			ACCT 335	MGMT 430	
		Visual			MRKT 230	MRKT 303	
To select and use appropriate and effective approaches and tools in solving a wide variety of problems	Problem Solving	Gathering Information			ACCT 201 FIN 380	ACCT 362	
		Problem Recognition			ACCT 202	MGMT 405	
		Creative Thinking			ACCT 321 MGMT 350	ACCT 322 CORP 320 MGMT 485	
		Systems Analysis			ECON 261	ACCT 370	
		Decision Making			FIN 380 MRKT 405	ACCT 361 MRKT 415 MGMT 425	
To look beyond one's immediate self and local community	Global Awareness	Works with Diversity			MGMT 460		498
		Understands Systems Interrelationships			FIN 350	MRKT 320	
To work together or act jointly to reach a common goal	Collaboration	Positive Interdependence			MGMT 330		
		Leadership			MRKT 305		
To select and apply technology appropriately	Technology	Selects					
		Applies			MRKT 302	FIN 375	

for ability-portfolio activities. Some faculty generated ability-based projects with rubrics and integrated them into their courses, while others created program maps that illustrated the connections between courses and the abilities and skills (see Table 1.2).

Abilities and Skills

Over the past eight years the faculty of Valley City State University have endeavored to modify the general education objectives and to establish a more meaningful connection between general education course work and the academic majors. To facilitate the process, a campuswide committee of faculty was formed. The committee identified a set of eight abilities from the existing objective statements and later added 22 skills that further defined the abilities. It was determined that students would demonstrate the abilities and skills through projects in both general education and major courses. These projects were constructed to include both content knowledge and experience in a specific ability and skill. The faculty reached consensus on the abilities and their related skills during the spring of 1999, with the completion and approval of the *Abilities, Skills, and Levels* booklet.

Documenting and assessing student growth in abilities became a topic of discussion on the campus. The senior portfolio assessment process is seen as a practical tool that allows students to demonstrate ability and skill competence levels.

Portfolio Integration

During freshman orientation, following the distribution of the notebook computers, a four-hour computer basics session is held. The senior portfolios are demonstrated at this time. Necessary hardware and software skills for multimedia development are included in a required general education course taken by 95 percent of freshmen. The course activities include Microsoft Office Suite, scanning, CD burning, and audio and video capture. All other necessary expertise is integrated into existing courses.

The division of education was the first to fully adopt the senior portfolio. Their graduates were required to present portfolios beginning in 2000. Beginning in the spring of 2002, all graduates from VCSU are required to present digital portfolios. Faculty in the students' academic major review and assess the portfolios. The completed portfolios are archived on CDs and stored in the university library. At the time of the portfolio presentations about 20 percent of students are asked to modify their portfolios prior to acceptance by the division. Many modifications are completed within a day, others are returned in a week, and, in the worst-case scenario, a student returns the portfolio after several months.

Each division determines how and where their students begin to develop the portfolio. Most have integrated it into a course in the sophomore year. All portfolios must demonstrate five abilities. The academic divisions determine which five of the eight abilities each major focuses on.

Each division offers a one-credit senior portfolio seminar to aid students in portfolio development. These seminars review portfolio expectations, the layout of the portfolio, the acceptable projects, and some of the technical skills required. In addition, a portfolio handbook for students is available. It includes step-by-step instructions, technical information, and examples. A Web site makes this document and other divisional materials available to students. (http://www.vcsu.edu/facultystaff-dev/portfolios.htm).

Problems and Issues

- During the first six months of the portfolio adoption process, the learning team met regularly to discuss the VCSU portfolio. The learning team focused on reading, reviewing, and discussing portfolio development. Hardware and software training for creating the portfolios was not begun until late spring of 1996. This planning period is very important because it takes the emphasis off electronic and places it on portfolio.
- The learning team struggled with how much of the portfolio should be prescriptive. The team reviewed many templates and looked at available samples from other institutions. Based on the VCSU's mission, the team envisioned a student-centered portfolio in which students make decisions on what and how to present the information.
- The team also encountered another portfolio difficulty. Too often portfolios became a collection of stuff (we use the metaphor "rattling shoebox"). A clear understanding of the purpose and use of the portfolio is important. Multiple purposes may cause it to become very cumbersome and difficult to assess. The team found its first choice of audience (employers) and purpose (employment) to be too limiting. In 1999, the decision was made to change audience to divisional faculty and purpose to academic assessment. Using the portfolio as an employment tool remains an option for students.

VCSU discovered the importance of mapping the projects in the various disciplines. This is the beginning of the assessment process and its importance should be realized. The maps effectively connect the outcomes of the major to the abilities and skills and provided students with a visual representation of how the portfolio projects fit into the curriculum. Table 1.2 is an example of a Business Administration map.

Tracking Student Progress

The university has come to realize the rich assessment potential of the projects. The senior portfolio encompasses only a small number of projects. However, it is necessary to collect and organize the projects before they can be utilized. Server space will soon be made available for students to deposit and store their projects. Like the senior portfolio, this space is to be managed by the student. The university has planned and is currently building a Web-based tracking software. This software will allow students, advisors, and faculty to track a student's progress through the abilities. It also provides an organized means of accessing projects based on student year, ability, and semester created. This access can provide evidence of student learning from freshman through senior year. The software was implemented in fall of 2003.

Evaluating Success and Assessing Outcomes

Faculty are diversifying the learning experiences of the students with innovative teaching strategies. Data gathered in 2000, the last year of the Title III grant, indicated faculty technology adoption was successful.

- 94 percent of faculty indicated they had portfolio projects integrated into their course requirements
- 80 percent reported their computer was essential to their teaching (Marcinkiewicz and Welliver, 1993)
- 69 percent of faculty reported they required students to use five or more types of technology in their courses

Data gathered over the five years of the portfolio adoption process (1996–2000) indicated growth in the use of technology for teaching and learning.

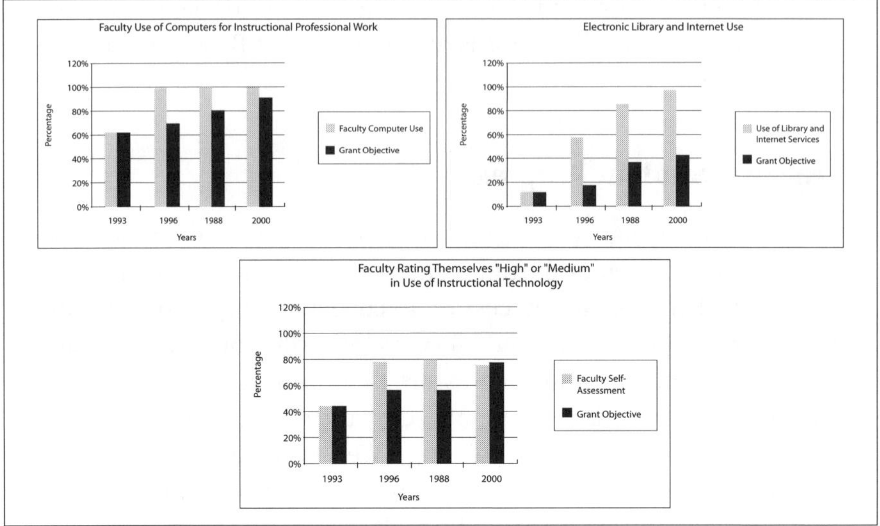

Figure 1.2 Comparison of Grant Objectives to Campus Data

- Percentage of faculty requiring student use of multimedia increased from 18 percent to 46 percent
- Percentage of faculty using multimedia in their instruction increased from 21 percent to 66 percent
- Percentage of faculty who included at least one technology requirement in their syllabi rose from 23 percent to 93 percent

Data from a faculty survey conducted by Kenneth Green in 1994 was used as baseline data for the Title III grant. The charts in Figure 1.2 represent the yearly grant expectations in comparison to VCSU survey results. The faculty's technology use met or exceeded the grant objective in every case.

Figure 1.3 compares the results of national surveys (Green, 1996 and 1999) on technology use by faculty to technology use by VCSU faculty. Technology use on the VCSU campus rose significantly higher than the national average between 1996 and 1999.

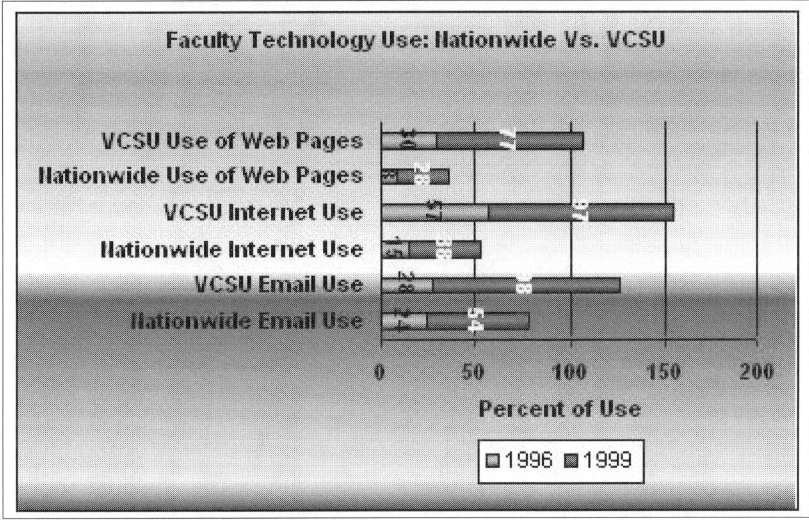

Figure 1.3 Faculty Technology Usage

Assessing Outcomes

- The ability-based projects that the faculty continue to create and improve provide richness in the curriculum that engages the students in more active, real-world learning experiences.
- The reflective statements required as part of the portfolios have affected the amount of reflective writing expected by faculty in other assignments.
- VCSU students are becoming self-directed, self-assessing learners. The use of ability projects in general education classes and the completion of the senior portfolio provide students with ownership in the assessment process. The student-centered tracking software for storage of projects will make students responsible for their learning materials.

VCSU has become a technology-rich teaching and learning environment. Student surveys reveal that the university is providing instructional methods that indicate good practices in teaching (Chickering and Gamson, 1987). See Figure 1.4.

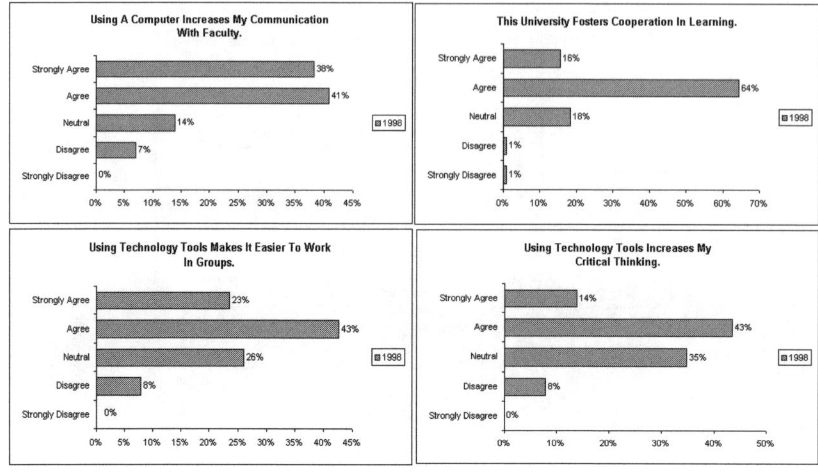

Figure 1.4 Student Survey of Good Practices in Teaching

Every year a survey is sent to employers of VCSU's newest graduates. The survey asks the employer to rate their satisfaction with the employee in each of the eight abilities areas. Figure 1.5 indicates the results of the surveys beginning in 1996. The charts display an increase in satisfaction by employers for nearly every year.

Over the five-year period from 1996 to 2000 four factors stand out as important in assessing the impact of the portfolios:

1. The student population attending VCSU has not changed during this period.

2. Campus surveys indicate technology use by faculty and students has increased significantly. The 1996 and 1999 Campus Computing Project surveys by Kenneth Green (http://www.campuscomputing.net) indicate that other institutions of VCSU's type have risen in the use of technology in instruction much more slowly than VCSU.

3. Students recognize that they are experiencing teaching strategies that indicate good practices in teaching (i.e., good faculty-student interaction, active learning, collaborative learning, and real-world applications).

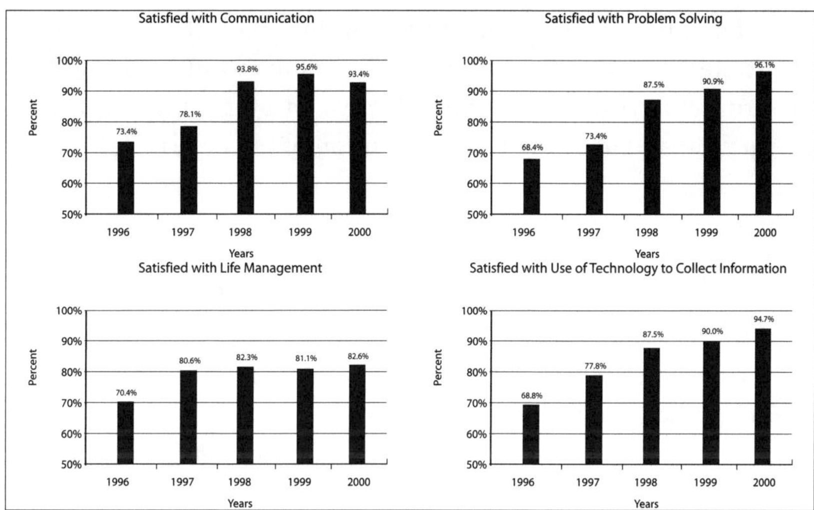

Figure 1.5 Assessment of Employer Satisfaction

4. The satisfaction of employers with VCSU graduates is increasing.

It is difficult to determine what part the portfolios alone played in the changes and improvements at VCSU over the past six years. It may not be necessary or possible to determine what impact the portfolio adoption had on teaching and learning. Researchers like Steve Gilbert (1996) suggested it is necessary to have a density of technology use before changes in learning can be appropriately measured. He states, "To make visible improvements in learning outcomes using technology, use that technology to enable large-scale changes in the methods and resources of learning. That usually requires hardware and software that faculty and students use repeatedly, with increasing sophistication and power. Single pieces of software, used for only a few hours are unlikely to have much effect on graduates, lives or the cost-effectiveness of education."

Once this technology richness is acquired it is only necessary to study the evolution of an institution's education strategies as Ehrmann (1995) states: "To assess changes in learning a university must study its educational strategies for using technologies. It is not possible to measure these strategies in a single course but it must be done across the institution or division if the evolution of the strategies is to be monitored." The results would indicate that electronic portfolios are an effective strategy for improving instruction and learning in an institution of high learning.

References

Chickering, A., and Gamson, Z. (1987). "Seven principles of good practice in undergraduate education," *AAHE Bulletin* (March). http://aahebulletin.com/public/archive/sevenprinciples1997.asp

Cole, D., Ryan, C., and Kick, F. (1995). *Portfolios across the curriculum and beyond.* Thousand Oaks, CA.: Corwin Press Inc.

Corwin, T. (2001). "Evidence of technology use at VCSU 1996-2000" (December, 2001) [Online]. Valley City State University, http://www.vcsu.edu/facultystaff-dev/research/researchonchange.htm

Ehrmann, S. C. (1995). "Asking the right questions: What does research tell us about technology and higher learning?" *Change.* XXVII: 2 (March/April): 20–27.

Gilbert, S. W. (1996). "How to think about how to learn." *AGB Trusteeship.* Special Issue 1996.

Gillespie, C., Ford, K., Gillespie, R., and Leavell, A. (1996)."Portfolio Assessment: Some questions, some answers, some recommendations," *Journal of Adolescent & Adult Literacy,* 36:6: 480–491.

Green, K. (1996). *Campus computing 1996: The seventh national survey for desktop computing and information technology in American higher education.* Encino, CA: Campus Computing Project.

Green, K. (1999). *Campus computing 1999.* Encino, CA: Campus Computing Project.

Holleque, K. (1998). "Validating the university mission: The learner survey." Unpublished survey and results reported to administration (November). [Online]. Valley City State University, http://community.vcsu.edu/facultypages/kathryn_holleque/Fall98Survey/Intro.htm

Marcinkiewicz, H., and Welliver, P. (1993). "Procedures for Assessing Teachers' Computer Use Based on Instructional Transformation." 15th Annual Proceedings of Selected Research Presentations at National

Convention of the Association of Educational Communications and Technology (New Orleans, LA), 679D684. Washington, DC: AECT.

Sheingold, K., and Frederiksen, J. (1995). *Linking Assessment with Reform: Technologies that Support Conversations about Student Work.* Princeton, NJ: Educational Testing Service.

CHAPTER 2

Secure, Scalable Proctored Testing for Online Students

Carole A. Hayes
Coordinator, External Relations
Office for Distributed and Distance Learning
Florida State University

Florida State University (FSU), a public Research 1 institution founded in 1851, serves approximately 30,000 students with a faculty of 1,500 full-time, part-time, adjunct, and visiting instructors.

FSU began offering online undergraduate degree completion programs for the fall 1999 term. The development of courses and mechanisms for student support were partially funded by a temporary legislative appropriation. This special funding was provided for three years and ended in 2002. The courses developed are available online, materials-based, and mentor supported. (For complete descriptions go to http://online.fsu.edu.)

At the outset of the online undergraduate degree-completion program offerings, Florida State University's Office for Distributed and Distance Learning (ODDL) solicited partners from among Florida's 28 public community colleges. At that time, no university had developed a model for integrated support services for online students. Therefore, FSU tried to anticipate the support functions online students would need and then sought to collaborate with local community colleges in providing these supports to FSU's online students. To that end, FSU negotiated a Memorandum of Understanding by which FSU would provide fully online courses leading to undergraduate degrees in computer science, information studies, nursing, and interdisciplinary social science, and partnering community colleges would provide specified student support services.

These degree programs offered online require that admitted students have at least the equivalent of the Florida Associate in Arts (AA) degree. They are *degree-completion* programs, providing upper-division courses only. This model was developed to benefit both Florida community colleges and FSU. Community colleges have been able to motivate current students and recruit new students by assuring them that after earning their AA degrees, they could earn an FSU bachelor's degree without relocating or quitting their jobs. FSU benefited by enrolling cohorts of students who had proven their abilities to succeed in higher education and who would be supported by institutions that had successful student support systems in place.

Community college partners would be paid $25 per credit hour for students in their service areas who were enrolled in FSU's degree-completion programs. The types of support anticipated were advisement, marketing, computer lab access, FSUCard photos, library use, optional local campus student activities access, and proctored testing. Eighteen of the 28 community colleges became partners; all others had options to participate at any time. Each term a survey was provided to partners asking for information about resources expended on FSU's online students in their area. Within three terms from the program's inception, the survey showed that the primary support service students used was proctored testing. Each of the other functions was provided for by statewide enabling policies or was simply not availed by students.

Partnering with community colleges to provide proctored testing resulted in three problems for FSU students and programs: scheduling the exams, delivering them to the testing proctors at community colleges, and having them returned to FSU.

Because academic schedules at community colleges frequently differed from FSU's, exam schedules often coincided with community colleges' spring breaks or with their summer schedules, when they were closed halftime or all day on Fridays. In addition, nontraditional (e.g., working adults with families) students often needed access to testing during evening or weekend hours, which were often not available.

Having the exam delivered to the proctor was another frequent problem the FSU program encountered. ODDL used Airborne Express for both the delivery of exams to proctors and the return of completed exams to FSU. Exams were often delivered to college mailrooms and were, therefore, not always delivered to addressees in testing centers in a timely fashion. If the addressees were not immediately available, coworkers might not open the envelopes or notify the addressees that they had been received. While these problems occurred relatively infrequently, as the number of courses and students increased the impact of the problems grew as well. The cost in materials, staff time, and postage for sending exam materials was high and growing higher. The community college staff would often ignore instructions about the return method for completed exams and use their regular postal mail system, which is untraceable and slower. Another possible occurrence was that a staff person would send the Airborne packages to the college mailroom where they might languish for days before entering the Airborne Express system and be on their way back to FSU.

Using Technology to Decrease Errors and Increase Efficiency and Efficacy

Enrollments have doubled each fall term since the inception of the fully online undergraduate degree-completion program in fall 1999. Consequently, the nightmares of nondelivered exams, fears of altered exams, and the cost of sending exams to hundreds of locations increased exponentially, and so FSU developed a solution to its proctored-testing problems based on available technologies. The new online system has benefited immensely the students, staff, and faculty participating in online degree-completion programs.

Instructors had been submitting their exams either as hard copies or e-mail attachments for ODDL staff to duplicate and mail. This process required multiple handlings of exam materials and resulted in a number of late deliveries and wasted staff time. The process also was not secure against exams being altered by one of the several people handling them prior to mailings and then again before they were administered.

FSU solved these deficiencies through an innovative method supported by online technologies:

1. Instructors offering courses with proctored exams format their exams in PDF—thus rendering them tamper-proof—and send them to a secure Web site to which only they and the proctored testing manager at ODDL have access.

2. The proctored testing manager uploads exams onto a password-protected Web site developed by ODDL's electronic campus coordinator.
3. Proctors are provided unique logins and passwords so that they may access their exams from this secure Web site. (This secure authentication allows each proctor access to only the exam(s) he or she is proctoring.)
4. The proctor prints the exam as needed; it is available only for a specific testing window, which is designated by the instructor.
5. The proctor administers the exam and then completes the certification of compliance with security procedures and acknowledgment of instructor requirements.
6. The proctor then sends these materials to FSU via UPS Campus Ship. (The proctor accesses FSU's online UPS Campus Ship account, prints out a return shipping label, and arranges for pickup of the exam[s] at no cost to the proctor or testing facility.)

In addition to making the exams secure from the point at which an instructor saves the exam in a PDF format until the instructor receives the completed exam, this system is also scalable: Because it is fully online, it is accessible to all approved proctors, without limiting the number of proctors or the locations of proctors. In addition, the cost of mailing packages to proctors has been eliminated completely. New problems occur as a result of the online access to UPS Campus Ship and some involve challenges in picking up materials from proctors. These have centered on the UPS Web-based shipment system. During spring term 2003 UPS revised the online process. The new system has technical difficulties that have caused some access problems, but this is being addressed by UPS and is improving.

How FSU's Online Students Locate and Get Approval for Proctors

The nearly exclusive use of community colleges for exam proctoring offered challenges that were addressed by designing and implementing a Web site to assist students, instructors, and proctors in coordinating secure proctored testing. The features of this site are:

- Information about what a proctor is, what a proctor does and who can be a proctor (requirements and necessary conditions)
- Proctor information on what is required and how to participate
- List of approved proctors
- Forms for Proctor Approval Application, Exam Certification, and completed exam cover sheet
- Advice and guidance to students on taking proctored exams
- Instructor information on how to prepare for an exam to be proctored

A group of ODDL staff members including the proctored testing manager, implementation manager, technical editor, external relations coordinator, an academic coordinator, and the associate director of ODDL worked to identify needs and design an information Web site to guide students in:

- Locating an existing proctor
- Locating a potential, appropriate proctor
- Obtaining approval of the proctor
- Determining the constraints of the proctoring situation, i.e., scheduling and fees (if any)
- Coordinating with instructors and ODDL exam facilitation staff

The site is organized according to three tabs: Student, Proctor, and Instructor. Each of these Web pages has a left frame listing questions relevant to the entire process with links to the answers.

The process includes finding a nearby proctor on the approved proctor list or finding a potential proctor from the clear instructions on who is and who is not acceptable for the job. A proctor approval application is provided as a Word document online for the student and proposed proctor to download and complete. This is submitted and reviewed by the proctored testing manager and two other staff persons. One of the requirements for proctors is that they have Internet access and the ability to print from electronic test files. As explained earlier, each approved proctor receives a login and password so that he may access the instructor's exams online from a secure site managed by ODDL staff. The proctored testing manager maintains files of proctors after verifying contact information and declared affiliation.

The site accessed by students, instructors, and proctors is http://online.fsu.edu/learningresources/proctoredexam. A visit to this site will fully demonstrate the student, proctor, and instructor experiences with the processes designed and implemented by ODDL (see Figure 2.1).

Implementation and Update

The implementation of these electronic support processes began in fall 2002. During that time, eight online courses were supported by the administration of 333 proctored exams to 62 students in the U.S., Puerto Rico, and onboard the USS *John F. Kennedy* by 76 proctors. The majority of students reside in Florida, but the same procedures, mechanisms, and logistical arrangements obtain no matter where the student is located. Approximately $3,600 was saved in duplication and mailing charges during spring 2003 alone. Problems encountered included some long printing times for proctors due to multiple pages in PDF, especially for mathematical materials, and procedural challenges with the return of completed exams via the UPS online scheduling and charge system. These problems were very minor and represented about 2 percent to 3 percent of all testing transactions accomplished during the fall term. During spring 2003, comparable figures were as follows:

- 13 online courses
- 183 students
- 600+ exams
- 6 countries (including the U.S.)
- 1 ship
- 104 proctors (59 of whom are new spring term)

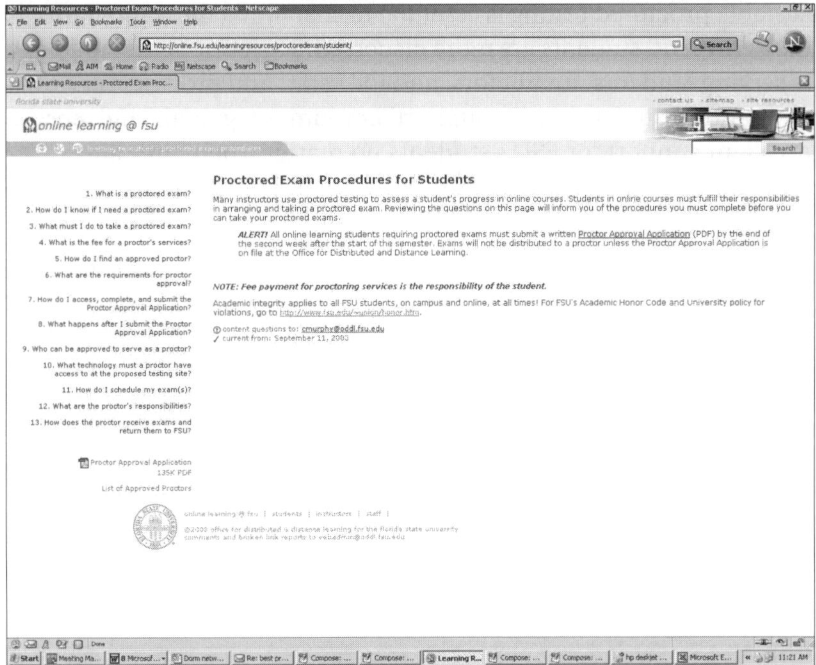

Figure 2.1 The Exam Proctoring Screen

A change in testing facilitation was piloted summer 2002. This change involves the transfer of proctored testing management to assessment services, a unit of ODDL. Since spring 2000, a staff person in the student support services group who also does student advisement and online student/course/program data management for multiple purposes has facilitated proctored testing. Assessment services handles all kinds of testing, on- and off-campus, as well as course and faculty evaluation. This reassignment is intended to be a more consistent use of resources to handle proctored testing facilitation by the unit that is designated for testing support. All of the earlier described processes will remain the same. Responsibility for facilitation of the processes will continue to reside within a different unit of ODDL with the conclusion of the successful pilot.

Enrollments have doubled each fall term since the inception of the fully online undergraduate degree completion program. Secure scalable proctored testing is essential to sustaining these programs as they grow and students are more dispersed. The current methodology is serving students, instructors, and FSU staff and proctors very well. It is anticipated to easily support enrollment growth and ensure excellent support for FSU's students no matter where they are.

Special acknowledgment and thanks go to Ms. Melanie Welch, Proctored Testing Manager/Online Program Data Manager/Student Advisor. Melanie has coordinated proctored testing logistics since spring 2000. She has guided all positive developments in the system and she carefully checked the use of facts and data in this chapter.

CHAPTER 3

The Associated Colleges of the South's Course Delivery System

Rebecca Frost Davis
Assistant Director for Instructional Technology
Specialties: Classics, inter-institutional collaboration
Associated Colleges of the South Technology Center

The Associated Colleges of the South comprises sixteen liberal arts colleges in twelve southern states. These institutions range in size of enrollment from roughly 900 to 3500. Incorporated in August of 1991, the ACS has a mission to make the case for liberal arts education and to strengthen academic programs of our member institutions through collaboration and technology.

ACS Course Delivery System

Beginning in Spring 2002, ACS commissioned the creation of a course delivery system (CDS) to facilitate Inter-institutional Collaborative Courses (ICCs) among ACS member institutions, which are taught partially online. Version 1.0 of the CDS premiered in Fall 2002, and version 2.0 was released in Spring 2003. In creating this system, ACS chose a tailor-made system over commercially available learning management systems (LMS). Although several ACS institutions use such commercial systems to deliver online course components, not all use the same one, so that inter-institutional courses cannot rely on a standard system being in place. Furthermore, ACS needed a system that consortium staff could administer, rather than relying on IT staff at participating schools. Large learning management systems, like Blackboard or WebCT, were out of the price range for these courses (which involve relatively few students and faculty), so the consortium first used a combination of WebBoard and a Real Streaming Media Server. When these commercial solutions proved unwieldy, ACS moved from a buy-it to a build-it approach for setting up appropriate courseware. As a result, the software used has similarities to many LMS systems but possesses crucial differences in emphases on real-time online lectures as a principal means of curriculum delivery, online student-student interaction and collaboration, and facilitation of inter-campus team-teaching. This build-it approach further strengthens our academic programs by driving the creation of a software engineering internship program in which ACS students design and construct software fitted to the needs of consortium members.

The key goal of the ACS Course Delivery System (CDS) is to allow instructors to remotely team-teach Inter-institutional Collaborative Courses (ICCs) over the Internet. This goal differentiates the CDS from many other learning management systems, which assume single instructors or that instructors and students in team-taught courses attend or teach at the same institution. Inter-institutional collaborative courses are similar to distance learning courses in that students participate in the course remotely from any ACS institution; they differ, however, from most traditional distance learning courses in that the teaching responsibilities are also distributed across multiple faculty on different campuses. This method exposes students at individual campuses to the expertise of faculty across all campuses. Furthermore, these Web-enhanced courses follow a hybrid model of e-learning through a combination of virtual interaction across the consortium and face-to-face interaction on each campus, where students work with a home-campus mentor. This hybrid model takes advantage of the learning tools offered by the Web, while preserving the liberal arts ideal of close, personal interaction between student and teacher. A typical ICC combines synchronous online lectures and discussions via a chat room with asynchronous course components, such as online readings, study questions, and exams. In order to meet the particular needs of this type of distributed learning environment, ACS needed a system that integrated streaming media and chat, provided the standard asynchronous elements, and helped coordinate multiple faculty.

Perhaps the most important tool in the CDS for facilitating ICCs is the Virtual Classroom (see Figure 3.1), where students and faculty meet for a weekly online lecture and discussion. This room integrates

Figure 3.1 Virtual Classroom, CDS 1.0. Links for selecting lecture notes and connecting to the audio stream are in the top frame. Lecture notes display in the middle frame. The chat room displays in the bottom frame.

Real Media live streaming, chat enabled by Macromedia Flash, and online course materials. By combining all of these features in one window, the CDS improves on the multiple windows and locations required when using WebBoard (the technology previously used by these classes), while hiding features, such as the threaded discussion, which are unnecessary for the live session. The CDS integrates audio streaming by automatically generating the link for the Webcast so that the technology is transparent to the users. The classroom displays HTML lecture notes and outlines in a center frame, while student interaction is handled by the chat room in the bottom frame. Participants may access previous or later lecture notes using a menu on the upper right. This feature allows them to make connections between different lectures. The designers modeled the chat room on Instant Messenger, a technology familiar to most ACS students. The main chat room is logged for later review, and the system also offers person-to-person chat, which, for example, support staff may use to deal with technical problems without disturbing the whole class.

Lecturers may also use the list of users in the chat room to check on class attendance. Typically, then, the lecturer delivers the lecture through the audio stream, while students ask and answer questions via the chat room.

Asynchronous features of CDS version 1.0 include a threaded discussion, class-wide e-mail (which is archived), on-line exams, and review of archived lecture sessions. ICC students use the threaded discussion to answer study questions that cover course readings and lectures. Faculty may designate a moderated discussion, in which student replies are held back until a moderator releases them, or an open discussion. The Session Archive, which is modeled on the Virtual Classroom, contains a link to the archived streamed lecture, faculty lecture notes, and a chat log from the live session. This feature is especially important since schedule differences between participating institutions sometimes prevent students from attending live sessions. The Session Archive also enables students to study archived lectures and chat discussions for exams.

The ACS Course Delivery System was originally designed to support courses for the Sunoikisis program, a collaborative program in Classics and Archaeology, which teaches three inter-institutional collaborative courses over the course of the academic year. Since the original design, ACS has continued development so that the CDS may meet the needs of other groups. Now the consortium supports the use of the software by any consortium member, and it is available for download under the GNU General Public License.

Based on the first two semesters of use and in order to meet the needs of expanded users, version 2.0 was released in the Spring of 2003 with the following goals:

1. increase the flexibility of the system for users;
2. reduce the time required to support faculty use of the application;
3. increase support for coordination of course activities;
4. increase opportunities for students to learn about, communicate with and work with other course students;
5. support the activities of mentors while trying to reduce their workload.

Several new or improved features answer these goals. First of all, the developers made the overall system more flexible by adding modularity. For example, when setting up a class, faculty can designate any or all of the available course modules (see Figure 3.2).

Modules:

module	yes	no	default?
Calendar	(•)	( )	(•)
Classroom Archive	(•)	( )	( )
Course Materials	(•)	( )	( )
Drop Box	(•)	( )	( )
Email	(•)	( )	( )
Exams	( )	(•)	( )
Roster	(•)	( )	( )
Study Questions	(•)	( )	( )
Todo List	(•)	( )	( )
Web Projects	(•)	( )	( )

ok reset cancel

Figure 3.2 Available Course Modules, CDS 2.0

Modules not chosen will not display when users visit this class. This feature allows a more tailored feel for the class and avoids confusing users with unused course components. For example Archaeology 111 does not have exams, but students who see exams listed on the course menu may be concerned that they have missed something. Modularity makes it possible for students to see only those modules they will need. Users may also take advantage of the Theme Manager to change the color scheme of their CDS. This flexibility in modules and display makes the CDS more accommodating, a characteristic important at small liberal arts colleges, which typically pride themselves on the unique character of their institution and faculty.

In order to support faculty use, the development team made more self-sufficient features in the system. For example, the new lecture builder allows HTML editing online without knowledge of HTML code. A media library facilitates the reuse of uploaded pictures or other media for lecture creation. Improved exam creation offers a wider variety of exam questions, as well as easier editing and reordering. Students may also submit work via a drop-box. The course documents builder permits faculty to add course documents in addition to the syllabus (which version 1.0 allowed). Finally, a context sensitive help system offers help geared to the location of the user within the course delivery system. All of these features empower course faculty and consequently reduce the time-commitment of support staff for this system.

In order to facilitate coordination between course participants at different institutions, which can be a logistical nightmare in these courses, designers have added a welcome screen with calendar and reminders for both students and faculty members (Figure 3.3). By using this system, a course director can manage both faculty duties, such as delivering lectures, and student assignments. This feature integrates information from the lectures, syllabus, discussion, and exam sections, which was already tagged by both date and course in the back-end database. A To-Do list feature provides further coordination of activities, especially for project management. The ability of the system to facilitate coordination between multiple campuses demonstrates its unique fit for use in the inter-institutional collaborative course.

The designers also sought to increase student interaction to fully take advantage of the multiple perspectives offered by Web collaboration. One strategy is simply supplying more information about users to other users. In addition to enhanced user profiles, there are course specific users profiles for which faculty can designate questions that pertain uniquely to the course. A second strategy for student interaction is a student collaborative workspace, where students from different campuses can upload documents and work on shared projects. Finally, increased student-student, as well as faculty-student interaction between different institutions, should lessen the demands on the home campus mentor for meaningful interaction. This strategy would then support home campus mentors and lessen their workloads.

ACS continues developing this project with impetus from multiple areas. Version 2.0 has been available for use since May 2003, and feedback from its users suggests new and improved features, such as the drop-box. Furthermore, ACS developers are working with developers of the Segue LMS at Middlebury College to coordinate features.

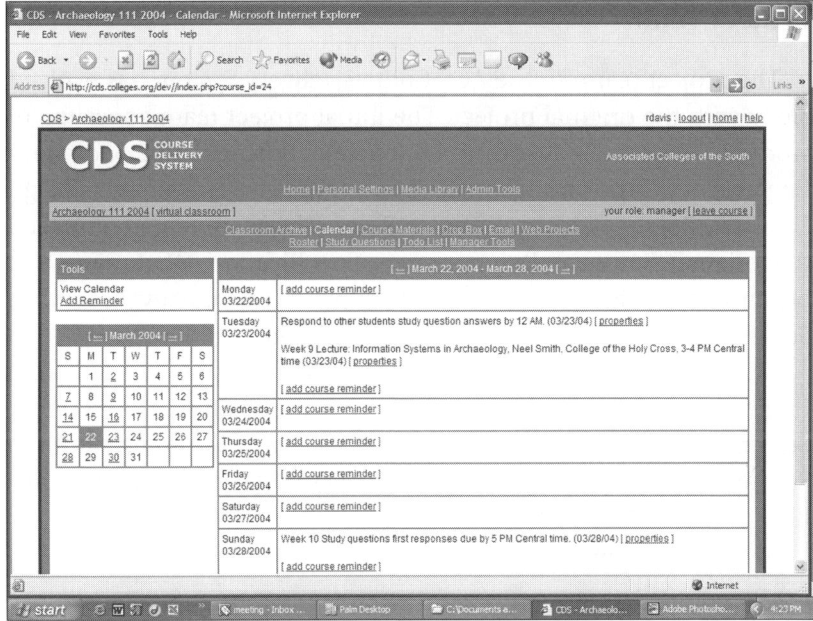

Figure 3.3 Welcome Screen with Calendars and Reminders, CDS 2.0

Segue, which was released in a 1.0 version in August 2003, is used by several small liberal arts institutions, including a pilot at one ACS institution, Southwestern University (http://segue.middlebury.edu/sites/segue). CDS and Segue designers have worked together under the auspices of NITLE (National Institute for Technology and Liberal Education). Segue's focus on liberal arts institutions as users makes it attractive for integration into the CDS. For example, Segue's Web publishing system forms the core of the Collaborative Student Project Space in the CDS. CDS designers welcome the creation of third-party course tools. In order to facilitate this integration, CDS designers have designed a modular system architecture that will allow outside plug-ins and ease future expansion of the system, also taking into account the need for interoperability with other external systems.

Project Team

The project team for the ACS Course Delivery System has evolved along with the original project. The initial project team consisted of students in Prof. Suzanne Buchele's Spring 2002 Software Engineering Capstone Course at Southwestern University: Leigh Lambert, Robert Reid, and Angela Roles. These students composed the original Software Requirements Specification Document and began coding the project. ACS Director of Technology Programs, Suzanne Bonefas acted as client for the project.

Development continued in Summer 2002 with the ACS Software Engineering Pilot Project under the supervision of ACS staff. Summer interns were Leigh Lambert, Angela Roles, Robbie Sternenberg, Zach Toups, and Joey Nasser. These students completed version 1.0 of the CDS.

ACS Staff on the project team include:

- ACS Technology Center Assistant Director for Systems and Development: Eric Jansson (Project Leader)
- ACS Director of Technology Programs: Suzanne Bonefas
- ACS Technology Center Assistant Director for Instructional Technology: Rebecca Frost Davis (User Support)
- ACS Development Specialist and Systems Administrator: Jason Jones
- ACS Postgraduate Software Engineering Intern: Karlie Verkest

In addition to ACS staff and interns, there has also been significant collaboration in development, especially with the team that developed the Segue course management and Web-content publishing system at Middlebury College. The Segue development team includes Alex Chapin, Gabe Schine, Adam Franco, and Dobromir Radichkov. The CDS and Segue teams have collaborated on a common Web application development framework, as well as common application services. In addition, both groups work with the Open Knowledge Initiative in implementing Open Service Interface Definitions (OSIDs).

Project Budget

The ACS has leveraged the already existing infrastructure of the ACS Tech Center to develop this project. Thus, most project expenses consist of staff salaries and come in two phases—development and support.

Development Costs

- 2 full time postgraduate interns (160 hours/month)
- 2 full time student interns (40 hours/week)
- 1 full time software engineering consultant (40 hours/week)

Support Costs

- 1/10 FTE user support
- 1/15 FTE systems administrator

Project Impact

The CDS has benefited not only its users but also the students who developed it and the consortium that conceived it. While the number of users is relatively small (total users by Spring 2004 are about 200), especially when compared with a campuswide LMS, the added benefits to student designers and ACS demonstrate the value of its creation. In essence, this project served as proof-of-concept for our hypothesis that ACS could develop a program that would prove beneficial to our computer science students by providing them with valuable applied software engineering experience as well as provide member institutions with custom-designed software. Students in future iterations of the program will also provide ongoing support and maintenance for software they create.

In the first year (AY 2002–2003), CDS 1.0 was used to varying degrees by roughly 50 students, 10 staff members, and 30 faculty. The system especially aided in the coordination of courses that had as many as 11 different faculty members from multiple institutions delivering lectures. All three Sunoikisis ICCs used the system:

- ICAGR395
- ICLAT395

- Archaeology 111

It was also used to facilitate communication between students in the Global Partners program in Turkey and students at DePauw University. Since AY 2002–2003 was essentially a pilot year, the number of users was small. Nevertheless, the system fully served the users for whom it was intended—Sunoikisis faculty and students engaged in inter-campus teaching and learning. The number of faculty impacted—30—is especially significant given the system's goal of coordinating the efforts of team-teaching faculty.

Version 2.0 has been available since May 2003. Since that time, in Summer 2003 it was used by 5 faculty members and 11 students participating in the Living in Yucatan course sponsored by Millsaps College, but with participation across the ACS. Also, faculty from 11 institutions used the system to prepare for, coordinate, and participate in the two Sunoikisis summer faculty and curriculum development seminars. These faculty continued using the system to complete development for the two Sunoikisis fall ICCs, which also used the system. Finally, 5 faculty members and 10 software engineering students from 8 institutions in a 9-week summer program used the system. Three courses were taught in Fall 2003. CGMA: GIS in Mediterranean Archaeology had 4 faculty members and 12 students from 4 institutions. ICAGR391: Homeric Poetry had 11 faculty members (from 8 institutions) and 11 students representing 5 institutions. In addition 18 other students, accessed some of the archived lectures as part of a separate English course on epic poetry. ICLAT391: Literature of the Early Republic had 11 faculty members (from 7 institutions) and 17 students from 3 institutions. There was some student and faculty overlap between the three courses. Finally, in Spring 2004, in Archaeology 111, 14 faculty members from 11 institutions are teaching 11 students from 6 institutions. The Living in Yucatan course has also expanded its use of the CDS to include some live lectures before the group departure, in addition to the sharing of materials that it did in 2003. This course has 5 faculty members and 13 students from three institutions. More and more, use of the system is expanding beyond traditional course delivery to inter-institutional collaboration. Furthermore, archived materials created for one course are being reused the next year by the same course (Archaeology 111 and Living in Yucatan) or by other courses (English students using archived lectures from Homeric Poetry).

In addition to the direct benefits to users, the ACS Course Delivery System has also benefited the students who designed and implemented it by offering significant real world experience in software engineering. Building on the success of the Summer 2002 pilot project, the consortium has established the ACS Summer Software Engineering Internship. In the summer of 2003, ten students from seven institutions came to the ACS Technology Center at Southwestern University to learn software engineering concepts and gain hands-on experience designing and coding real world applications. This internship featured a hybrid approach that combined more traditional software engineering elements with extreme programming (XP) principles. The program ran from June 7–August 9, 2003, during which time students were in residence at the ACS Technology Center. The software engineering interns produced a Digital Assets Management System (DAMS) named DAMSEL. For more information about this product, please visit: http://dev.colleges.org/typo3/damsel.0.html. The software was designed to meet the needs of the REALIA project (www.realiaproject.org) a collaborative project of Modern Languages faculty within the ACS. The summer internship will be offered again in Summer 2004.

This model of software development offers much to a consortium of small liberal arts colleges. Beyond the freely available software, the model also can strengthen the offerings of computer science programs, which are traditionally stronger at large universities than small colleges. These improved programs mean that computer science majors can both experience a liberal arts education and gain a competitive education in computer science. At the same time, the consortium benefits from the students' work. This model fits into a larger strategy of using undergraduate resources, e.g., through internships, to compensate for the limited resources of a small college.

Finally, the creation of the CDS has benefited ACS staff members by enabling us to participate in a dialogue about academic information systems in a way that would be impossible if we had not had the experience of creating this system. Just as there was an explosion of administrative systems in higher education, more recently there has been an explosion in academic systems. We are better able to meet the needs for information about such systems because of our experience with the CDS. Moreover, we are better able to advise our constituents in making strategic decisions. The combined benefits to users, developers, and consortium staff make the CDS a truly important contributor to the

ACS mission of enhancing liberal arts colleges through technology-enabled collaboration.

What Would We Do Differently if We Were Starting Over?

Overall, ACS is very satisfied with how this project has proceeded. As with most projects, however, there is always some room for improvement. For example, project leader Eric Jansson says, "I would make it more configurable for users." That is, he would give the users more options in how the system looked and in arranging their resources and classes the way they want to create a sense of unique identity by class. Such flexibility fits the character of small liberal arts institutions. At the same time, Jansson concedes that this direction is more dangerous for developing and using such a system because it exposes the user to more complexity which detracts from ease of use.

Jansson also identifies the need to learn more about what products other users at the university were using and the relationship between those products and the CDS. Questions to consider include:

- What other products are users familiar with? For example, do they use a commercial or other learning management system, such as WebCT or Blackboard? Do they use a digital assets management system?
- How does the CDS fit in with other products the prospective users know? What role does it play vis-à-vis these systems? Does it provide services that they do not need? How can we make the CDS complementary to products already in use? Can the CDS interoperate with these other systems?

Finally, Jansson identifies several new directions the project has taken since its inception. The designers have implemented a more scalable framework based on the Model-View-Controller design that will more easily accommodate future expansion and ease maintenance. In an effort to explore ways to better integrate the software within different campus environments, they have met with the Open Knowledge Initiative (OKI) developers, a team developing a set of middleware software interfaces that define standards for accessing the back-end administrative databases and services of a campus (http://web.mit.edu/oki). The CDS team has been involved in efforts to explore using OKI Open Service Interface Definitions (OSIDs) from within the PHP environment. They have also focused their efforts on interoperability, especially under the auspices of the Open Knowledge Initiative (OKI). Since a developers meeting with OKI in Spring 2003, ACS developers have been implementing OKI Open Service Interface Definitions (OSIDs). Finally, they have also created a more modular system so that faculty users may tailor the system to the particular needs of their classes. In addition to choosing the theme (display color scheme and layout), these users may also designate which modules their courses should contain, e.g., study questions, exams, etc.

Project Evaluation

Evaluation of this project has been based primarily on actual use. CDS 1.0 went through beta testing in August 2002. Then it was used for three courses in AY 2002–2003. Success depended on functionality (the ability to deliver multiple courses in one semester) and ease of use for all users and was evaluated by informal user feedback, as well as course evaluations. Both measurements have demonstrated the success of the project. Most importantly, the technology has become essentially transparent for the users.

Version 2.0 entered beta-testing in Summer 2003, with full implementation in Fall 2003. Success has been measured by the same criteria as version 1.0. Course evaluations for two of the courses were designed and analyzed as part of a three year evaluation of the Sunoikisis program, the ACS program that most often uses the CDS. Numbers of complete evaluation are relatively small, so statistical analysis is difficult (5 for the ICAGR391 and 11 for ICLAT391). Still, with results taken from the larger sample, the Latin course, these evaluations do demonstrate the success of the CDS as a tool for inter-institutional course delivery. Respondents were asked to evaluate the ease of use and functionality of the following features: audio lectures, archived lectures, Web resources, and the online discussion conference. All responses for these technical questions averaged over 4 on the Lichert scale (1–5). Now that these survey instruments have been created, they will be used in future Sunoikisis courses and will provide us with more data about the CDS. Furthermore, anecdotally, support time for the system also seemed less to support staff in Fall

2003. Once again, both measurements demonstrated a successful project. In addition, the expansion of use beyond inter-institutional courses into workshops and other areas demonstrates an added measure of its flexibility.

Success for the CDS has also been determined by the impact of this project on student designers. The success of the Summer 2002 pilot project has led to the creation of the ACS Summer Software Engineering Internship. This internship drew applications from twenty-five applications from twelve ACS and one NITLE (National Institute for Technology in Liberal Education) Southern Region institution. The number of applicants and the range of ACS schools demonstrates the need this program fills for computer science in liberal arts institutions.

Lessons Learned and Advice to Other Institutions

From this project, ACS has learned valuable lessons about software design, the role of students, and collaboration. First of all, the creation of the course delivery system has taught us that if commercial solutions do not offer the best fit for an institution's need, the build-it approach is feasible. At the same time, small institutions must think creatively in finding resources to design their own software. Often students are an untapped resource. As Jansson explains, "They are really good at what they do; they take instruction well; they learn from each other." Large research institutions typically rely on graduate students for such work, but small liberal arts colleges do not have that resource. We have found, however, that the undergraduate student can also be a valuable resource for such projects. On the other hand, student developers do need some guidance; that is, they need access to some experience in software development. That guidance could come from a variety of sources, e.g., software engineering faculty, software engineering consultants, or IT staff with software development experience. The model established by ACS—combining software engineering curriculum with developing experience in a student internship—benefits both students and the institution. In fact, this opportunity makes our institutions more attractive for prospective computer science students.

Institutions may also look beyond their own students and staff for help with developing software. Inter-institutional collaboration is part of our consortium's mission, but this project led us to look outside ACS for partners in software development. ACS designers have worked closely with two groups: designers of the Segue LMS at Middlebury College and the Open Knowledge Initiative (OKI). The CDS and Segue teams have collaborated on a common Web application development framework, as well as common application services. Work with OKI has ensured compliance with developing standards for LMSs. Both of these relationships have stimulated the creative energy of the ACS team and helped ensure the viability of the CDS in a broader environment. In particular, compliance with industry standards will facilitate expansion and interoperability with other systems. While collaboration has been greatly beneficial to this project, often software engineers, especially those with experience in commercial environments, are hesitant to participate in this type of collaboration. As Eric Jansson explains, "The opportunities for collaboration in a corporate environment are so restricted, but in this environment the opportunities are real. I was skeptical going into these meetings, but now I am convinced that because this is an academic environment this is a productive way to spend resources in a university. I think collaboration can work." By taking advantage of this unique aspect of the academic environment, ACS has been able to find a successful model for software development at small institutions.

For more information about the ACS Course Delivery System, please contact Rebecca Frost Davis at rdavis@colleges.org or (512) 864-5664.

CHAPTER 4

An End-to-End Solution for Internet Lecture Delivery

A. C. M. Fong and S. C. Hui
School of Computer Engineering
Nanyang Technological University

Introduction

Declining costs of computing power, coupled with the phenomenal growth in Internet usage, have created much research interest in the development of Web-based communication systems. Internet delivery of educational materials across vast geographical distances becomes an attractive alternative to the traditional modes of communication, such as mail, phone, and fax, for on-demand learning.

There has been much debate on the usefulness of the Internet for educational purposes. For example, Bork and Britton (1998) have concluded that the Web is still not suitable for teaching. In Vouk et al. (1999), the authors highlight the shortcomings of current Web-based teaching applications. These include poor end-user quality of service (QoS) and lack of interactivity. The principal problem is that earlier use of the Internet for educational purposes had focused mostly on putting supplementary teaching materials on designated Web pages. In Maki (1997) the authors adopt readily available resources, such as the textbook publisher's demonstration software, to reduce the students' equipment needs.

Recently a number of encouraging studies have been reported. Tian (2001) concludes that the Web is a cost-effective technology to facilitate the development of educational applications. The benefits of Web-based teaching extend well beyond classroom materials. As described in Bazillion and Braun (2001), the classroom, library, and other campus resources can be linked up into a single educational network. The lack of interactivity problem has been addressed in Chu (1999), where a real-time interactive feedback mechanism is proposed. Also, Bedell and Somers (1999) have reported an automated tool that facilitates immediate student feedback to the instructor and other students.

However, the full potential of the Internet for teaching purposes can only be realized when multimedia applications are deployed in a Web-based environment. In fact, a number of domain-specific applications have been reported. For example, Crutchfield and Rugh (1998) have developed interactive demonstration and exercise modules for the study of elementary control systems.

With Web-based multimedia teaching applications, students only need to have access to a Web browser to participate in teaching activities. However, the current best-effort Internet is a harsh environment in which to transfer audio and video data due to severe bandwidth, packet loss, and delay constraints. Also, the network condition can be unpredictable and time varying. In this chapter, we describe how we tackle the technical problems and present an end-to-end solution for delivery of "live" and recorded multimedia lecture sessions over the Internet.

In the next section we describe three popular commercial video delivery systems, highlight the technical challenges involved, and explain the motivation for a customized solution. Then we discuss the technical problems involved in the delivery of audio and video information over the Internet. We also describe current approaches to such problems. Next we present our end-to-end solution based on a one-to-many server-clients topology. We also describe an integrated approach to the Quality of Service (QoS) problem. The integrated approach combines network congestion control and error control into a single mechanism. We then present performance analysis of our Web-based solution and then present our conclusion.

The School of Computer Engineering (SCE) is one of the five engineering schools in the College of Engineering (http://www.ntu.edu.sg/coe), the other schools being the School of Civil and Environment Engineering, the School of Electrical and Electronic Engineering, the School of Materials Engineering, and the School of Mechanical and Production Engineering. One of the world's largest engineering colleges with 14,000 students and 1,600 staff, the College of Engineering aims to promote greater synergy in cross-disciplinary teaching and research by building a common platform that draws on the key strengths of each school.

Commercial Video Delivery Solutions

Currently, the most popular commercial video delivery solutions include QuickTime (Apple, 2001), Windows Media (Microsoft, 2001) and RealVideo (RealNetworks, 2001). Although QuickTime and RealVideo support a variety of platforms (e.g., Solaris, Linux, and Windows), the Windows Media server only runs on Windows and the client only supports Windows and MacOS. The oldest of the trio, QuickTime was first released in 1991. It is now supported by more applications than any of its competitors (Lawton, 2000). However, a survey has shown that QuickTime is mainly favored by Macintosh users (CNET, 2001). Although RealVideo's strength lies in its highly scalable design, Windows Media's main strength is its easy-to-use interface for Windows users. Windows Media also reportedly provides the best audiovisual play-out quality (CNET, 2001).

One fundamental problem with all these commercial solutions is that they are optimized for high bandwidth connections (Lawton, 2000): 500 kbps for RealVideo 8, 700 kbps for QuickTime 5, and 720 kbps for Windows Media 7. However, a useful solution for students is one that minimizes the client side equipment overhead requirements, which implies the need for a low-bandwidth solution optimized for 56 kbps modem connection. In addition, all commercial solutions require the installation and subsequent updating of client side applications/plug-ins for different platforms. Our goal is to provide students with a Java-based solution that they can use to access the system anywhere with any Java-enabled Web browser on any platform.

There are three key technical challenges involved in the development of an end-to-end multimedia delivery solution for low-bandwidth operations: Interoperability, Compression, and Internet Congestion (Lawton, 2000).

Interoperability: Currently, there is no standardized format, and our goal is to develop a platform-independent solution using Java technology.

Compression: This is absolutely essential, particularly for low-bandwidth applications. Currently, only Windows Media uses MPEG-4.

RealVideo uses a 2-pass compression algorithm that is effective in reducing data redundancy, but incurs up to 20 percent delay. Our goal is to support generic multimedia data by considering techniques from a transport perspective rather than a semantic perspective (Wu et al., 2000).

Internet Congestion: Users of commercial delivery products are well aware of their limitations in delivering high-quality video, especially with low-bandwidth connections. Common solutions to transmission interruptions provided by commercial vendors tend to focus on infrastructure solutions. For example, companies like AboveNet Communications and Digital Island circumvent the congestion problem by selling access to their high-bandwidth networks (Lawton, 2000). In our research, we focus on robust QoS control that does not rely on the network to provide QoS support. This approach is most suitable for heterogeneity between different platforms and across different portions of the Internet.

Quality of Service: Problems and Approaches

The Internet provides a continuously available communications medium for near-instantaneous transfer of information across vast distances. However, there are many problems associated with high-bandwidth applications such as transmission of video and audio information as there are severe constraints on bandwidth, packet loss, and delay that affect the perceived quality of video play-out. In addition, the network condition is both unpredictable and time varying. Another problem is that the Internet is heterogeneous in nature. This problem arises because different portions of the Internet have different resource-management strategies with respect to storage, bandwidth, etc. Finally, we have quality assurance problems associated with the current Internet Protocol version 4 (IPv4). Its best effort strategy does not provide any QoS guarantees. Although the emerging IP version 6 (IPv6) has been designed with network-layer QoS capabilities in mind (IPv6, 1998), it is unlikely to completely replace IPv4 in the foreseeable future (Durand, 2001).

Thus, we must provide QoS guarantees at a level higher than the network layer. This entails employing QoS mechanisms at the application layer. Currently, application-layer QoS control involves two mechanisms: network congestion control and error control (Wu et al., 2000). The purpose of network congestion control is to ensure optimum usage of prevailing network resources. This means we aim to match the transmission bit rate (and hence the quality of the audio/video signal) to the available bandwidth. Network congestion control involves three steps: rate control, rate shaping, and rate adaptive coding. In rate control, the transmitter and/or receiver estimates the available bandwidth. Rate shaping then adjusts the transmission bit rate accordingly. In addition, rate adaptive coding provides a means to adjust the quality of the transmitted signals based on a rate-distortion (R-D) tradeoff (Ortega and Ramchandran, 1998). Error control mechanisms provide extra error-resilience to channel errors while the data are being transferred. Currently, there are two major error control approaches: retransmission and forward error correction (FEC). Retransmission is efficient, in the sense that redundant data for error recovery are only sent when packet loss has been detected at the receiver. However, the delays incurred in resending error recovery data are generally unacceptable to multimedia applications, particularly when real-time delivery is required. FEC is currently the most promising error control approach.

In addition to the more conventional QoS mechanisms described earlier, some techniques involve the reservation of resources to guarantee reliable delivery of audio/video data (Braun, 1997). However, these approaches tend to be over conservative and therefore often lead to suboptimal resource usage.

End-to-End Solution

From this discussion, we set out to develop a Web-based multimedia lecture delivery system based on the one-to-many server-clients topology. Our system is designed such that a number of students can simultaneously request for "live" or recorded lecture play-out via a client application launched from a Web browser. In addition, we employ a sender-based FEC mechanism that provides the necessary robustness against channel errors. In our FEC scheme the number and nature of redundant parity packets are adaptable to the prevailing network condition at each receiver. When a receiver detects any occurrence of transmission errors, it can use the redundant information to recover the lost packets without incurring any additional transmission delay, as shown in Figure 4.1.

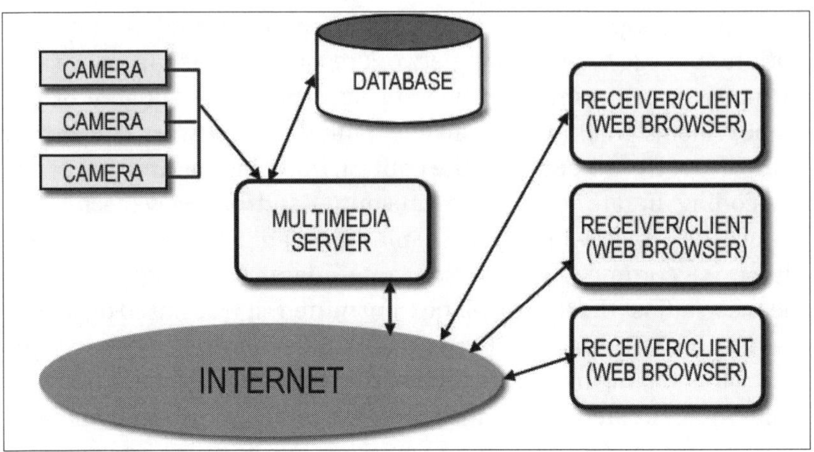

Figure 4.1 End-to-End Multimedia Lecture Delivery System

The server performs the necessary compute-intensive processes, such as rate control estimation, that provide the required QoS guarantees. This approach reduces the equipment overheads and latency at the client side. From Figure 4.1, preinstalled cameras (with microphones) first capture raw video and audio data in lecture theaters, and send the data to a multimedia server. Initially, we only have one multimedia server. To enhance subsequent system scalability, each multimedia server is designed to handle cameras in one geographic location (e.g., all lecture theaters in one building). The data are then compressed using the MPEG-4 standard so that the server can support VCR-like functions such as play, pause, rewind, and fast-forward. The compressed data may be archived in a multimedia database, if required, for later retrieval. Each multimedia lecture sequence is suitably tagged for subsequent identification. A tag may contain the following information:

143.473 Adv Image Proc L6, Object Segmentation, 10 Aug 2001

If a student requests for a lecture play-out, one of two scenarios can happen. If "live" lecture play-out is requested, then the multimedia server will take the raw video/audio signals from the appropriate lecture theater, compress the data, perform the necessary QoS control and Internet transport processes, and transmit the information to the client via the Internet. The client application then performs error recovery (as appropriate) and MPEG decompression. On the other hand, if recorded lecture play-out is requested, the multimedia server first retrieves the relevant compressed data from its database. The other processes are the same as in the "live" case. In either case, an exchange server (not shown in Figure 4.1 for clarity) provides the necessary directory and IP resolution services, and session control (e.g., negotiation and termination). This reduces the burden on the multimedia servers, so that these servers can be dedicated to handling audio and video data.

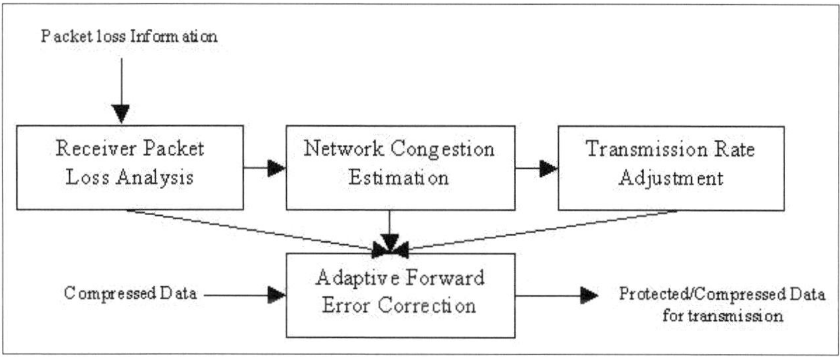

Figure 4.2 Processes of IQCM

Figure 4.2 shows a schematic of our integrated QoS control mechanism (IQCM). It is a four-process mechanism that performs the tasks of network congestion control and error control. Each receiver gathers packet loss data and transmits the data to the multimedia server for analysis. Based on the analysis, the server performs network congestion estimation and rate adjustment. All this information is then used to adjust the amount of redundant recovery information appended to the video/audio data, these data are then sent to the corresponding receiver.

We have developed a simple-to-use interface that users can launch using any Java-enabled Web browser. The interface provides VCR-like buttons for enhanced usability. A student can first use the directory service to find the desired "live" or recorded lecture session under the "Window" menu. Next, the student may adjust video settings (e.g., camera angle) under the “Video” menu. In the future we intend to allow the end-users to record partial video sequences locally if desired.

Performance Analysis

To gauge the effectiveness of our end-to-end solution we have conducted a number of experiments to measure packet loss rates and the level of user satisfaction. We found that a packet rate of more than 25 percent would lead to poor perceived quality of multimedia lecture play-out, whereas a loss rate of less than 10 percent was considered to be good. Using five Pentium II 400MHz PCs with 128 megabytes RAM running Windows 98 (one as multimedia server and the others as clients), we conducted our experiments from 10 AM to 11 AM (period of high network usage) and from 10 PM to 11 PM (relatively low network usage). Each video session lasted 10 minutes. The experimental results are illustrated in Figures 4.3 and 4.4, respectively.

In Figure 4.3 the initial network condition was very poor and resulted in a high packet loss rate of more than 30 percent. The QoS control mechanism responded and brought the loss rate down to within the acceptable band of between 10 percent and 20 percent. At the 420th second there was a sudden and significant increase in the loss rate to slightly above 20 percent. This was probably due to an

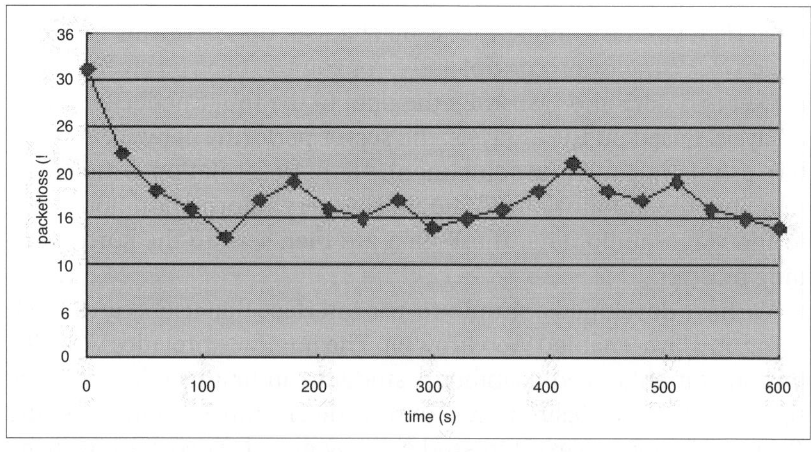

Figure 4.3 Packet Loss Rates During Heavy Network Usage

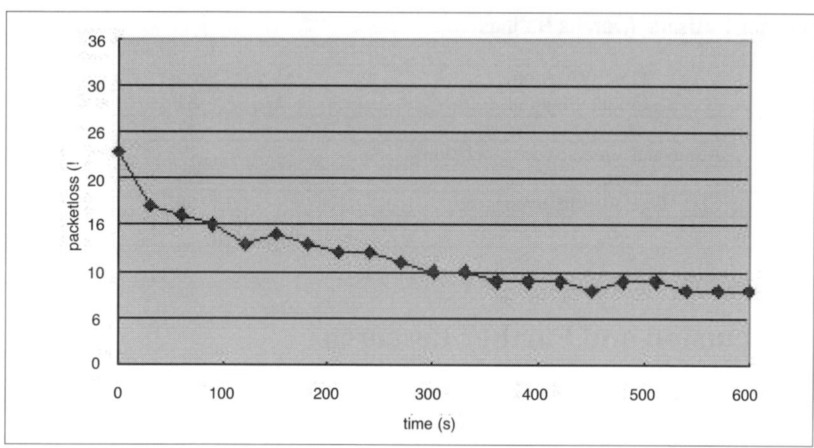

Figure 4.4 Packet Loss Rates During Light Network Usage

increase in network usage by other users. Figure 4.4 illustrates a gradual reduction in packet loss rate from an initial 23 percent to a little below 10 percent, which resulted in good play-out quality. Overall, Figure 4.4 shows a less fluctuating curve than Figure 4.3. We conclude that our packet loss rate consistently ranged from just under 10 percent to 20 percent under both network conditions. The perceived quality of lecture play-out therefore ranged from "acceptable" to "good," and was considered "fairly good" most of the time.

End-users' perceived quality of a multimedia delivery system is at least as important as objective measurements. Thus, we have also asked six volunteers to randomly test and rate our system based on criteria such as perceived lecture play-out quality and speed of response. Table 4.1 summarizes the results of this subjective test. In Table 4.1 video and audio qualities are considered separately. Synchronization refers to how well the video and audio signals coincide with each other. The response time measures the time it takes to receive the play-out data following a request. Each tester was also asked to give an overall rating on the system. We conclude that the initial results are quite encouraging. With 56 kbps modem connection, users have reported that our system is less susceptible to quality degradation caused by network interruptions as compared to popular commercial systems.

Table 4.1 Users' Average Ratings

Quality Measure	Average Score (100 max)
Video Play-out	83
Audio Play-out	85
Audio and Video Synchronization	
Response Time	93
Overall Effectiveness	88

Conclusion and Further Research

In this chapter we have outlined the motivation for adopting the Internet as a communications medium for educational purposes. In particular we have highlighted the opportunity of using the Internet for delivery of "live" and recorded lecture sessions. However, the Internet is a harsh environment for transmission of audio and video data due to severe constraints on bandwidth, packet loss, and delays. Also, the best effort nature of current Internet does not provide any QoS guarantees. Thus, we have presented an end-to-end solution for on-demand Internet lecture delivery with an integrated application-layer QoS control mechanism. Our system is based on a one-to-many server-clients topology that allows several students to access lecture sessions simultaneously. There is relatively little equipment overhead on the client side. In fact, students only need to use a standard Web browser to launch the client application. Results from initial tests conducted have been encouraging. Further system enhancements have been planned to incorporate user-interactivity allowable by the use of MPEG-4 video object planes (VOP).

References

Apple (2001). http://www.apple.com/quicktime

Bazillion, R. J., and Braun, C. L. (2001). "Classroom, library and campus culture in a networked environment," *Campus-Wide Information Systems*, Vol. 18, No. 2: 61–67.

Bedell, L. R., and Somers, M.D. (1999). "CyberInteractor – a teaching and research tool," *Campus-Wide Information Systems*, Vol. 16, No. 1: 17–23.

Bork, A., and Britton, D.R., Jr. (1998). "The Web is not yet suitable for learning," *IEEE Computer*, Vol. 31, No. 6: 115–116.

Braun, T. (1997). "Internet Protocols for Multimedia Communications, Part 2: Resource Reservation, Transport, and Application Protocols," *IEEE Multimedia*, No. 4: 75–82.

Chu, K. C. (1999). "The development of a Web-based teaching system for engineering education," *IEE Engineering Science and Education Journal*, Vol. 8, No. 3:115–118.

CNET (2001). Software Reviews, http://www.cnet.com/software

Crutchfield, S. G., and Rugh, W. J. (1998). "Interactive learning for signals, systems, and control," *IEEE Control Systems Magazine*, Vol. 18, No. 4: 88-91.

Durand, A. "Deploying IPv6," *IEEE Internet Computing*, Vol. 5, No. 1, Jan.–Feb. 2001: 79–81.

IPv6 (1998). "IPv6 QoS Implementation," Information available online at http://www1.ietf.org/mail-archive/ietf/Pre_Oct_1998/msg01117.html

Lawton, G. "Video streams into the mainstream," *IEEE Computer*, Vol. 33, No. 7, July 2000: 12–17.

Maki, W.S. and Maki, R.H. (1997). "Learning without lectures: a case study," *IEEE Computer*, Vol. 30, No. 5: 107–111.

Microsoft (2001). http://windowsmedia.com/download/download.asp

Ortega, A., and Ramchandran, K. (1998). "Rate-distortion methods for image and video compression," *IEEE Signal Processing Magazine*, Vol. 15, No. 6, Nov. 1998: 23–48.

RealNetworks (2001). http://www.realnetworks.com/products/servers/server8.html

Tian, S. (2001). "The World Wide Web: a vehicle to develop interactive learning and teaching applications," *Internet Research: Electronic Networking Applications and Policy*, Vol. 11, No. 1: 74–83.

Vouk, M. A., Bitzer, D. L., and Klevans, R. L. (1999). "Workflow and end-user quality of service issues in Web-based education," *IEEE Trans. Knowledge and Data Engineering*, Vol. 11, No. 4: 673–687.

Wu, D., Hou, Y. T., and Zhang, Y-Q (2000). "Transporting real-time video over the Internet: challenges and approaches," *Proc. IEEE*, Vol. 88, No. 12; 1855–1875.

CHAPTER 5

Professors at Charleston Southern University Get a Lesson of Their Own—In the Latest Computer Software

Mollie Gore
Staff Writer, University Relations
Charleston Southern University

On the final afternoon before spring break in April, 2003, the classroom filled up slowly: a few students arrived on time, but others dragged in well after the clock struck one o'clock.

Finally, the professor addressed the assembled students, all staring intently at their open laptops and today's lesson, an introduction to Microsoft Access.

"Click on the start button," Professor Larry D. Smith began. As the lesson progressed, there were the usual befuddled scowls and outcries of "wait!" and "how?" But this was no usual class.

The students in the Charleston Southern University (CSU) classroom were all full-time professors. They included the dean of the CSU School of Business and one of the computer science professors. Collectively, though, they were a microcosm representing the curious predicament facing colleges and universities around the country today.

For professors over the age of 25—and virtually all of them are—computers were most likely not a big part of their own learning processes in high school and college. But today's employers expect college graduates to be familiar with modern hardware and software, and students coming to college today expect to use more sophisticated technology than that which they used in high school.

Furthermore, students expect their professors to know more than they do—not just regarding the history course they're taking, but in respect to the technology they're using to learn. And as the professors at CSU are finding out, technology goes a long way in making courses more interesting and understandable to students, increasing their performance in the course and their success at college.

Charleston Southern University is the second largest private, accredited university in South Carolina. It offers more than 35 undergraduate and graduate degrees, and its fall 2004 enrollment approached 3,000 students. Although CSU has a traditional liberal arts curriculum, it has evolved into a university where students pursue a number of professional degrees. It is the only private university in the state with a master's degree in criminal justice, for example, and it has one of the state's best teaching schools—at the graduate and undergraduate levels. Its growing bachelor's degree in nursing is well respected, as are its premed program and other science-heavy degrees. The school's mission is "promoting academic excellence in a Christian environment," and it is affiliated with the South Carolina Baptist Convention. That mission statement drives everything the University does, and it is responsible for many of the innovative programs and approaches on the campus today.

Student success, in a nutshell, is the driving force behind CSU's renewed commitment to technology, a commitment that took a giant leap forward in October 2002 with the receipt of a $1.8 million U.S. Department of Education grant. The faculty members who gathered that Spring Break Eve illustrate the level of buy-in among professors to this campuswide commitment.

At some level, before professors can teach technology or use technology resources in class, they must learn.

"We have faculty members who are all over the scale as far as the computer skills they possess," said Larry Smith, who is in charge of CSU's technology training program. "There are some who can teach me things." And Smith admits there are others who aren't sure where the "start" button is.

This particular group of professors is familiar with computers, but not necessarily with the latest software in use today. Their teaching areas range from computer science to business to English. They've been chosen as a peer group to be trained first, and then they will train their colleagues, who will train their colleagues.

These professors have the best to work with: a "smart" classroom filled with new laptops, software, and accessories all bought in 2003, thanks to that $1.8 million federal grant CSU received in October of 2002. The grant is also paying for upgrades in the university's general computer labs, and it is helping fund key personnel to provide the hands-on training and maintenance.

Smith runs through the basic language of Access. A database is made up of tables, which include records of fields filled with characters, he says. Dr. Arnold Hite, dean of the school of business and a student today, frowns and looks at Smith.

"This file is a dot-D B S?" he asks, his brow furrowed.

"Dot-M D B," Smith answers patiently.

Sitting in the corner of the room, Dr. Bill Bowers, professor of business policy, waves his hand wildly. "As an instructor, when would I want to use a database?"

Smith answers him and moves on, explaining the nature of tables that relate to each other in Access. "It's like Legos," he says. "You just keep building on. Are you with me?"

A few more frowns dot the faces of his students, who sit silently.

"Trust me," Smith says.

Two hours later, the professors-turned-students shut down their laptops and leave for the weekend. Hite, the business dean, said he has a lot of experience using Microsoft Excel in class, and he likes it. He is no computer novice. But "this is hard for me," he said of the new software program. "This is more than you can remember."

The Title III Grant for Technological Advancements is funding for five years (2002–2007) what CSU calls Project ImPACT (*Im*proving *P*rograms *A*cross the *C*urriculum through *T*echnology). Already, the money has significantly enhanced CSU's efforts to fully utilize computer-assisted instructional techniques in the classroom. Project Impact is expected to drive higher student retention and graduation rates by offering an education that integrates top-shelf technology into the teaching and learning processes through faculty training, hardware and software episodes and course development..

Specifically, the money is split between faculty training and technology purchases. Approximately half the funds are devoted to the faculty peer-training program, with the seed group of professors highlighted here learning to use the new equipment. The training spreads out like ripples on water as the faculty talk about success and train others, until the entire university faculty is reached and any technology gap is effectively bridged.

An existing classroom already has been converted into the Project ImPACT Technology Teaching and Learning Center for faculty and staff. The center showcases the latest applications for teaching and will serve as an ongoing faculty-training center. Through training workshops like the one described earlier, as well as private consultations, demonstrations, and exhibits of software and hardware, faculty will come to understand—and, more importantly, apply—effective and efficient uses of technology.

The rest of the funds are allocated for equipment to provide state-of-the-art learning environments for students, faculty, and staff. As the grant progresses, several "smart" classrooms will be equipped with laptops and wireless Internet access.

A note about wireless Internet use: CSU was the first university in the greater Charleston area, and one of the first in the country, to offer its students free wireless access to the Internet from their residence halls in 2001.

In 2001, there were just 150 residential students at CSU using Internet access, which was then available through a dial-up connection. By 2003, more than 600 students were using the system, which became saturated. Compounding the problem: since it was a dial-up system, students using it from their dorm rooms had to choose between their phone and their computer, and dorm rooms house two or more students—and one phone line.

Not surprisingly, last spring one of the biggest student complaints at CSU concerned the speed and availability of Internet access. Over the summer of 2001, CSU's administrative services department supervised installation of the equipment necessary for wireless service, and students returning that fall received a wireless access card—free of charge so long as the card is returned in good condition when they leave for the summer.

CSU President Jairy C. Hunter, Jr., summed up the potential for Project ImPACT this way: "Our students will be the ultimate winners, because they will be taught by faculty who are trained in new technology, and they will learn in state-of-the-art 'smart' classrooms." He cut the ribbon on the Project ImPACT center in December 2002. The equipment installed in the room includes a document camera, a projector, a digital camera, a projection screen, portable carts of laptops that can turn other classrooms into "smart" learning centers, and other computers, printers, video and audio equipment, and accessories.

Although the emphasis in 2003 was on faculty training, the Project ImPACT center already is being used by some professors to teach their classes of students. Dr. Timothy Saxon, assistant professor of history, is midway through a semester of Western Civilization II, and he is teaching in a way that most people couldn't have imagined as recently as the 1990s.

Dr. Saxon gave lectures on a comparison of two European famines and an introduction to Europe after the Napoleonic Wars. The oddest thing about the class: these history students watched his presentation the entire class—and they took no notes. Instead, the students interacted with the professors and students, discussing events and debating the lessons needed to learn from history.

Dr. Saxon lectured against a backdrop of colorful, animated Microsoft Power Point slide shows. There is text—his outline—decorated with editorial cartoons from the period, or full-color portraits of the historical figures they are discussing.

When the class studied the French Revolution, students logged onto the laptops at each of their desks and surfed the Net to the site of George Mason University (GMU). GMU has Web pages devoted to the French Revolution that would have been of no help to CSU students in the 1980s without a bus to transport them to GMU in northern Virginia and a couple of days to spend in the stacks there. And the virtual tour Dr. Saxon's students took of the Palace of Versailles another morning would have required—well, an airplane and a lot of money.

The trip these students took during their study of the International Revolution was back in time: they visited a BBC site that offers several "working" inventions from that era. The students were able to see the work and even take the machines apart to see how they operated—virtually, of course.

History class isn't what it used to be!

Beyond the revolutions offered during class, this technology is offering students a break from the writer's cramp syndrome that often afflicts history students. Dr. Saxon posted his Power Point show on the CSU intranet, and he e-mails each week an outline of his lectures to each of his students. He encourages the students to view the slide show before each class, and this facilitates the in-class discussion.

Students take some notes of their own, of course—on the laptop, so they can e-mail their notes to themselves or save them on a disk—but they don't have to worry about getting every date and every fact down, and that enhances their actual absorption of the lesson, according to Dr. Saxon.

The Title III Grant for Technological Advancements ultimately will allow CSU to have eight "smart" classrooms. It will also allow for the purchase and use of three mobile carts of laptops and other equipment that can be used in any CSU classroom and across all of the university's disciplines. In addition to equipping the first center, CSU has already bought 32 new computers to upgrade its labs in the Derry Patterson Wingo School of Nursing and in the Master of Business Administration program.

"The bottom line is, the students are going to benefit," President Hunter told the audience in attendance at December's ribbon cutting. "We have two goals: to retain more students and to help students graduate and be successful."

Figure 5.1 Computer Science Instructor Jacqueline H. Hundley, left, and Business School Dean Arnold J. Hite sort out a setback during a recent computer class.

Project Impact came about through the efforts of many at CSU, but the primary architects were Chief Information Officer Rusty Bruns; Dr. Pat Bower, professor in the School of Education; and Dr. Mary Gene Ryan, dean of planning and student success. Dr. Ryan is the project coordinator.

"We're very excited about the possibilities this grant is affording us," Dr. Hunter said. "We're able to focus our efforts across the campus, so as our graduates move out into the real world they will be equipped to do research, to find information they need, and to communicate on a global basis."

CHAPTER 6

An Outward Design Support System to Increase Self-Efficacy in Online Teaching and Learning

Peggy E. Steinbronn and Eunice M. Merideth
Drake University

Introduction

Scott stares glumly at the computer screen that tells him to download the document from the course he is taking online, open it inside the browser with an appropriate application, respond to it, save it as an RTF file, and upload it onto the Web. "Huh?" Meanwhile...Dr. Madeline Wade waits impatiently for her students' responses and wonders: "Did they get the e-mail with the file attachment? When did these other two students show up? How do I know if they are legitimate registrations? What if...?" Although these two Web users seem to be on opposite sides of a learning environment, what they both have in common is a feeling that they are lost, and their self-efficacy is diminishing rapidly.

Self-efficacy refers to the conviction that one can control her outcomes and do what is necessary to produce a certain result. As early as 1977 Bandura established that this sense of control and belief in what one can and cannot do establishes "how much effort people will expend and how long they will persist in the face of obstacles and aversive experiences" (p. 194). When applied to learning, early success contributes to self-efficacy that then supplies motivation to persist. Motivation enhances problem solving, which then influences later success.

Increasing self-efficacy for both online teachers and learners means strengthening the chances of early success in a technological format, which is both a product and a process. Distance education exists because of human ingenuity, yet humans are often intimidated by the means of accessing that education. Designing support that helps both faculty and students start strong and stay engaged in online situations can build confidence and empower creativity. Successful online support, after all, should positively impact the psychological and physical environment of teaching and learning in an electronic arena and influence the retention rate of students.

White and Weight (2000, p. 69) report the following reasons for students who drop out or stop out of an online class:

- students leave because of isolation
- students leave because of the accelerated pace
- students leave because of competing responsibilities
- students leave because of technical issues

Although these reasons are compelling for students, they also deserve serious consideration from a faculty member's point of view because isolation, pace, competing responsibilities, and technical issues can singly or together create an environment of anxiety and frustration about control and ability. In addition, Chang (1998) maintains that for faculty "technology must be consistent with their existing values, and there needs to be a real educational value beyond the use of technology for its own sake" (p. 1). Faculty members, therefore, also need support in the planning and design of course content as well as time considerations to undertake and implement different strategies for online learning. Copying and pasting lecture notes into a Web page may reproduce the material, but these processes do not reproduce the interactive communication and engagement that can be promoted with live nonverbal expression and body language.

The purpose of this chapter is to present an Outward Design System for online support of a Web-based summer program that has been implemented at a medium-size liberal arts university where student-involved learning is at the heart of the mission, and technology is an important part of the vision of the institution. Because a sense of personal agency or self-efficacy may be the most important determinant of motivation, the needs of both the teacher and learner need to be considered and integrated into the design and implementation of online support for teaching and learning.

To design this type of support system, one begins at the center of the Online Support Needs Diagram (see Figure 6.1) to make sure that the core of the support system—the connectivity—is firmly in place. The support design then moves outward to enable maintenance, creativity, and the construction of meaning. Because the emphasis is on early success, support cannot be generated only as crises occur; support for the shared and unique needs of the stakeholders should be identified and in place before the implementation of online instruction whenever possible. The reality of teaching and learning in any environment, however, is that support is never static. It must continue to evolve to meet new needs.

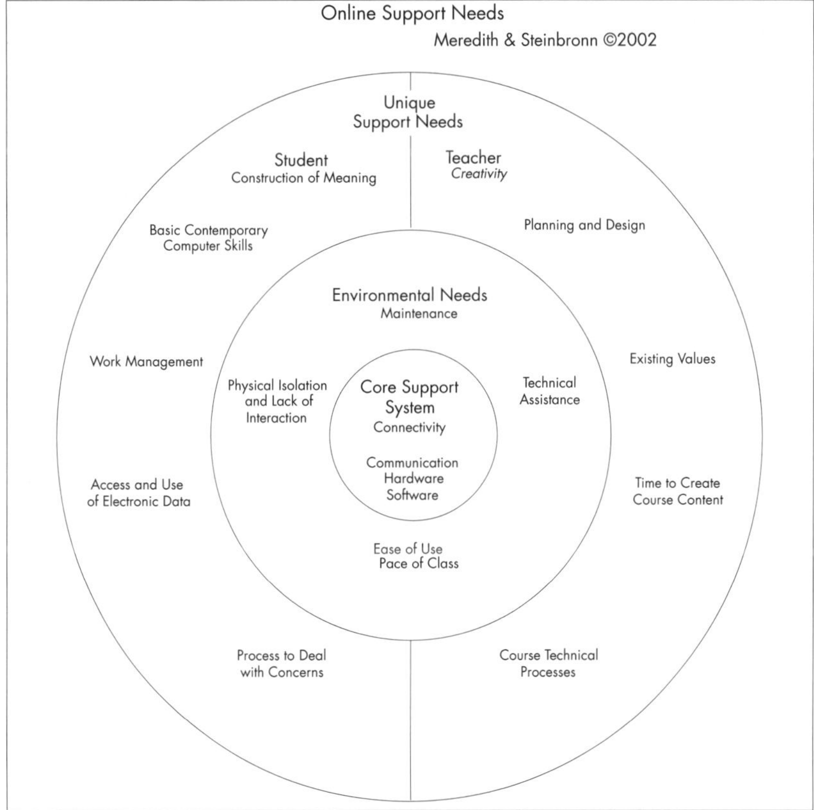

Figure 6.1 Outward Design System for Online Support Needs

Core Connectivity Needs of All Stakeholders for Online Support and Self-Efficacy

The Outward Design for Online Support ensures that communication, computers, servers, and software will be functional and provide interfaces for both humans and machines. Online teaching does not require less communication, but even more communication of specific information that recruits students and then keeps potential students interested and motivated. All stakeholders also need server reliability and 24/7 accessibility to be able to function in an "anywhere anytime" environment. Computer considerations must be clear to all stakeholders from the start; distinct hardware parameters are necessary for productive connections. The type of operating system, browser levels, and plug-ins needed to successfully navigate the site and comply with Web software should be identified for all users so that learning the content is facilitated and not blocked by technical considerations. Web education software defines the look and feel of the courses, so maintaining a balance between the powers of consistency and flexibility is important for any user's sense of control.

Serving a variety of stakeholders who have shared connectivity needs requires creative strategies to address different levels of need with different levels of support. For the purposes of this design, the levels of support are measured by how much support is given and the effort incurred in producing and maintaining that support. For example, the following levels of support address core connectivity needs for online teaching and learning.

Level 1 = Promotional communication that is interesting but doesn't overstate the realities of Web-based education. This communication would include a clear description of system and browser requirements as well as time considerations for the users and the process to attach, send, and receive text documents on the World Wide Web.

Level 2 = Web-based directions with visual aids (screen shots) for setting browser preferences and configurations with directions about how to correct any technical deficiencies with issues that can be anticipated. Periodic e-mails to students who have indicated interest; also, encourage and inform prospective students and faculty alike about the possibilities and processes of Web-based education.

Level 3 = Server accessibility (24/7) and a well-maintained Web infrastructure are not luxuries but necessities for this level. In addition, this level would require strong hardware and software support for faculty. Finally, electronic mailing of Web course areas and descriptions to other universities and listservs promotes registration and a support for marketing on a more national scale.

Environmental Online Support Needs

A basic concept within the theory of self-efficacy is that motivation can be learned. By helping teachers and students recognize and address shared needs, control and motivation of all users are both enhanced for the specific experience and "learned" for future online experiences. Gage and Berliner (1988) assert, "what is important here is matching the environment to motivation patterns" (p. 359). The shared needs of students and faculty are environmental—physical and psychological isolation, the pace of the course, and the perceived ease of the technology. These academic and personal environmental needs are factors in maintaining the course. Hatcher and Craig (1998) acknowledge environmental needs when they warn, "isolation can lead to a de-humanizing of the learning experience" (p. 4). Obviously, then, special care must be taken to design and support the ease of use of course materials and interactivity between students as well as between students and faculty online. Chickering and Ehrmann (2000) find that this is not only possible, but that interactive communication strategies that strengthen the shared environment can actually empower students.

Electronic mail, computer conferencing, and the World Wide Web increase opportunities for students and faculty to converse and exchange work much more speedily than before these technologies were available, and more thoughtfully and safely than when confronting each other in a classroom or faculty office. Total communication increases and, for many students, the result seems more intimate, protected, and convenient than the more intimidating demands of face-to-face communication with faculty (p. 1).

Different levels of support to further environmental goals include:

Level 1 = Publication of an introduction to the course and a short online syllabus at least two months before the beginning of the class. This preview allows students to understand the workload of the class and to obtain textual materials prior to the first day of the class. The online introduction and syllabus also focuses the faculty member's continuing Web course design, so that the course is not created "ad lib" shortly before student use.

Level 2 = Demonstrations of different types of assignments and class management tools to create interest and increase efficiency. Some interactive activities, however, may involve more "help desk" calls as students seek support for something new. For example, initial introductions, collaborative and cooperative group work, case studies, simulations, and role-playing are all possible using forums, chat rooms, white boards, and even e-mail. Assisting faculties in the use of management tools to enter grades, students in posting to portfolio files, and both faculty and students in providing feedback also contributes to creating a positive climate for a virtual classroom for students and faculty.

Level 3 = Instructor-to-student and student-to-student communication structures calm frustration and enhance learning for everyone involved. The technology that allows faculty to specify communication-rich assignments (team projects, required discussions, "guest speakers," peer editing, or peer presentations with responses) is available. However, this level of Internet use will also call for increased support because it also implies different avenues for completion of these assignments. Both students and instructor will need to understand how the "group" function in an Internet evironment works, how to electronically exchange files, when to use a synchronous or asynchronous discussion board, and how editing functions in word processing can be utilized. Short tutorials about these types of functions can be made available through Web links within the course. While these more sophisticated means of communication are more time consuming than simple read-and-response assignments, they also lead to better exchanges. Moreover, they allow students and instructors to expand their technological skills.

Unique Support Needs by Web Faculty for Online Support

Unique support needs are no less real or less important than shared environmental needs. These are, however, more difficult to anticipate, so planning for support that increases self-efficacy for faculty demands ingenuity and collaboration. Web faculty are often encouraged when they find that many good things that they do in a face-to-face classroom will work for online instruction. On the other hand, they must be willing to leave the lecture behind and think in terms of interactive and active learning approaches to keep students engaged. This transition takes reflection and some technological skill and creativity, but it is also supported by formal professional development workshops and time. Sherry, Billig, Tavaline, and Gibson (2000) maintain that faculty who will be Web teachers need to have time for training as well as "demonstrations of promising practices and ongoing professional development by peers" (p. 45). Teachers need to know what is possible and has been successful before they can begin to envision their own successful design. Faculty members' thinking about technology-based learning is influenced both by their perceptions of the goals of education and their comfort with the instructional technology that empowers students to reach those educational goals. The unique support needs of faculty, therefore, include the planning and design of the course content and its technical context, the faculty member's existing values, and time scheduled for help when developing the course. Support strategies that address these needs include:

Level 1 = A novice-level workshop about technology integration that encourages a KISAC (Keep It Simple and Creative!) approach. When faculty understand and begin creating their courses with a universal design in mind, they will not have to spend valuable time editing and re-entering course materials. In addition, mounting on the Web a faculty help page with frequently asked questions can help share information among instructors and provide faculty support that may be accessed multiple times without intimidation or embarrassment.

Level 2 = In-depth workshops in a number of time slots about Web pedagogy and the software that supports it to meet a variety of faculty teaching schedules. In a virtual environment, faculty members cannot depend on students understanding what is intended or the nonverbal feedback that often signals student anxiety or confusion. Faculty members must make connections between Web course content and Web course goals and expectations with specific directions and published criteria for assessment. In order to create and activate the course, faculty members must know the strengths and limitations of the software they are using so that they can plan interactive activities and assessments that will work in the course software environment. In addition, directions and criteria for assessment must be clearly communicated to the user.

Level 3 = "Hands-on" workshops about page design and image manipulation. With course plans in place, faculty members require support in making their Web courses interesting and their classes learning communities. Uploading visual materials that conform to Web standards and that are American Disability Act (ADA) accessible, internal linking to other sites, and creating quizzes and tests online are more sophisticated tasks and need lab time and direction. Some faculty members who are just starting may need one-on-one support as they begin to work with technology. On the other hand, faculty members who are advanced users may need help as they seek to incorporate new technologies. A faculty open-lab, available for development two hours weekly, creates an opportunity to drop-in and find help. This support system cannot give faculty release time, but it can make sure that faculty time is a respected resource and used well.

White and Weight (2000) assert that, "effective online teaching is twofold: the ability to transmit messages clearly and accurately and the ability to maintain positive interpersonal relationships" (p. 10). If faculty members are to be effective teachers and feel they are in control, then they must have the support to develop the knowledge and confidence to show enthusiasm both for their content and for distance education.

Unique Support Needs by Web Students for Distance Education

The fact that the World Wide Web makes it easier to deliver anytime/anywhere teaching material is irrelevant if students find the technology cumbersome, or if they are not appropriately supported in their attempts to learn with it. Making the technology as user-friendly as possible is the first step toward supporting their self-efficacy and promoting success. Students need to know how to manage browsers and plug-ins that will be needed to successfully navigate the site. Basic computer skills are essential. However, students have needs that go beyond the computer hardware and software, but which affect technology. They also need information about time and work management of online learning: Does the potential student like to read and write? Can she type? More than one student has found that electronic communication means a level of typing that he had not envisioned.

Palloff and Pratt (2001) assert that, "successful online students demonstrate good thinking skills, an ability to work and do some amount of research independently, and an ability to work with a minimal amount of structure" (p. 109). From this perspective, students also need assistance to help them use electronically accessed data productively. This productive independence empowers students to construct their own meaning for information, thereby creating cognitive connections and directions that have more relevance for them as individuals. This may mean online training and information to aid them in securing material through electronic databases, interlibrary loans, government archives, news services, etc. As students progress through a course, easily accessible technical assistance should be available and a structured system needs to be in place to address student concerns and complaints. Students want convenience, and they want "a curriculum that integrates theory with practice while emphasizing workplace competencies along with teamwork and communication skills" (Klor de Alva, 2000, p. 37). To accomplish these goals, the Outward Design System creates the following levels of support:

Level 1 = Clear information about the dates the class will be held, how to obtain course materials and textbooks, and a hyperlink to an online student guide for the software and a preliminary syllabus.

Level 2 = Technical support for students on the Web through an e-mail contact page. Other types of assistance would include specific help pages about submitting assignments, accessing grades, and participating in multilevel discussions. Periodic e-mails with a newsletter format alerts students to important deadlines as well as university policies and procedures. Students will often read a friendly e-mail while ignoring an official announcement.

Level 3 = Immediate technical help with an 800 number or periodic help through office hours in a real-time chat room. Whatever the media, questions directed to support personnel must be answered accurately and quickly. Establishing an electronic peer mentor network in a Web-based environment also allows students to interact online with peers who have taken Web courses previously so they might seek academic and technical advice. Moreover, the university using the Outward Design System has initiated a course site for all students so that they might seek the appropriate level of support, as they need it. This site functions as a performance support system that gives information as it is needed and presumably as it is used "just-in-time." This information is provided in a series of learning units with the following topics:

- Navigating Blackboard—directions and information about navigation properties and processes to be successful as students pursue their courses
- Blackboard Communication—directions and information about communicating with the instructor and other students in courses
- Assessment and Online Grading—directions and information about turning in assignments to be assessed and finding course grades in Blackboard
- Special Applications—directions and information about special applications used in online courses (for example, directions and links for downloading Adobe Acrobat, using media plug-ins, and special student tools)
- Online Learning Resources—online learning resources available through the university library

As students register for any course, they are added into the performance support site with a standard username and password so their support site is as visible and easily accessed as their course site.

Assessment of the Outward Design System for Online Support

Any design process needs assessment to test its strength in implementation and provide information for refinement or restructuring. This design for online support is informed by data from student evaluations of Web-based courses for the summer sessions 2000 and 2001. The return rate from Summer 2001 was 287 of 781 students or 37 percent. Because the return rate of this survey was still relatively low, these figures must be viewed only as indications and are not generalizable. The information about registrations and students, however, form a profile of continuing growth that is important to support considerations (see Table 6.1).

Even though the number of novice users is declining, it is declining slowly. The number of respondents who have never engaged in

Table 6.1 Web Program Growth Indicators

Year	Registrations	Number of Students	Number of Courses	Number of Survey Respondents	No Web Course Previously
Summer 2001	1017	781	53	287 (37%)	68%
Summer 2000	817	624	49	270 (43%)	76%

online learning is still large enough that it impacts the amount and levels of support needed. The items on the 2001 program evaluation survey that addressed the particulars of technical support had mixed responses:

- 74 percent of the respondents felt that the Drake network or Drake technical problems did not affect the ability to access courses
- 41 percent of the respondents found help pages useful, but 56 percent did not use them
- 24 percent of the respondents found the help desk or online technical assistance helpful (74 percent did not use the help desk)
- 94 percent of the respondents were satisfied with ease of online registration
- 93 percent of the respondents were satisfied with timeliness of registration confirmation

Technical implications for future support planning was informed by the following Summer 2001 data:

- Technical Connections (56k modem—43 percent; cable—22 percent; 28k modem—18 percent)
- 97 percent of the respondents knew how to attach files to e-mail
- 98 percent of the respondents knew how to upload and download files
- 90 percent of the respondents' computers support audio
- 85 percent of the respondents' computers support video

Besides the types of technical support needed, the survey was also able to obtain data that indicated when students were more likely to work online and need access to electronic support and/or support personnel. Respondents indicated a real preference for evening work as described by the times they were most likely to work on their courses below:

Weekday mornings	9 percent
Weekday afternoons	9 percent
Weekday evenings	31 percent
Saturday A.M.	9 percent
Saturday P.M.	11 percent
Sunday A.M.	10 percent
Sunday P.M.	20 percent

These times made the levels of online support all the more important, but the hours of the help-desk personnel were also adjusted to compensate for the heavy evening use.

The last and very important question of the survey asked respondents if they would take another Web course at this university. A resounding 86 percent of the respondents from 2001 said yes, up from 84.8 percent in the summer of 2000, and 72 percent in the summer of 1999. Obviously, the Outward Design Support System cannot claim sole responsibility for such a positive response, but it has contributed to online success and satisfaction among students.

Future Directions

Online teaching and learning currently involves radical changes in our traditional paradigms of academic thinking and acting. Newer areas such as streaming audio and video will also require the continuing evolution of support systems. By focusing on the success and control needs of the stakeholders involved in online teaching and learning, teacher and student self-efficacy and, therefore, active participation can be accomplished and sustained. The following areas will undoubtedly affect online teaching and learning, "pushing and pulling" online support in new directions:

- Bandwidth and speed of data transfer—The segment of the Internet that brings course material into a student's home or the faculty member's office will continue to increase in capacity and speed. These possibilities also bring the problem of infrastructure support and standardization of hardware memory and speed in configurations.
- Availability of hardware and user-friendly software—The dot-com culture of virtual e-commerce and education is influencing the price of Web-based hardware and software, bringing it to a level that is affordable by the average user. Support in this area involves a continual learning and teaching of new technologies and new pedagogies that best exploit the strengths of the new technologies.
- Limitations of specific hardware and software—All applications and the equipment needed to run them have both advantages and limitations in design and operation. Testing applications before students encounter problems can indicate support that may be needed. Help pages that answer projected concerns can streamline the technological context of online learning, making the content the focus of the course.
- Synchronous learning systems—The ability to log on and to interact in real time with an instructor and/or other students will moderate the amount of text currently required. This advance, however, requires support for those students across time zones and with varying access speeds.
- Consumer demand—Students are turning to distance education for convenient anytime, anyplace educational experiences. In doing so, the learner must assume responsibility for more independent learning. However, consumers also assume that online institutions will have support available "just in time" to meet their immediate needs.
- Economic factors—Students may be able to avoid travel, and/or on-campus residency, thus reducing educational

expenditures. In addition, students can continue to work as they learn because they are not governed by a university class schedule. While this is a benefit for students, it also creates the need for electronic support outside of regular office hours and 24/7 access.

- Sophistication of Web faculty—As higher education personnel become familiar with new software, and digital peripheral equipment, they will need more server space, speed, and support in maintaining advanced techniques as well as the quality of educational experiences throughout the course.

A successful design for distance education support does indeed involve different levels, numerous strategies, and its own measure of resources. Some support needs of online teachers and learners are shared; others are not. However, all of these needs are real and must be part of an Outward Design Support System for online teachers and learners if self-efficacy is to be achieved.

References

Bandura, A. (1977). *Social learning theory.* Englewood Cliffs, NJ: Prentice Hall.

Chang, V. (1998). *Policy development for distance education.* (ERIC Document Reproduction Service No. ED423922).

Chickering, A. W., and Ehrmann, S. C. (2000). *Implementing the seven principles: Technology as lever.* Retrieved July 25, 2002, from www.tltgroup.org/programs/seven.html

Gage, N. L., and Berliner, D. C. (1988). *Educational psychology* (4th Edition). Geneva, IL: Houghton Mifflin.

Hatcher, T., and Craig, B. (1998). *Humanizing the technological learning experience: The role of support services as socialization in a human resource development distance education program.* (ERIC Document Reproduction Service No. ED415-407).

Klor de Alva, J. (2000). "Remaking the academy." *EDUCAUSE Review,* March/April, 32–40.

Palloff, R. M., and Pratt, K. (2001). *Lessons from the cyberspace classroom: The realities of online teaching.* San Francisco: Jossey-Bass.

Sherry, L, Billig, S., Travaline, F., and Gibson, D. (2000). New insights on technology adoption in schools. *T.H.E. Journal*, 27(7), 43–46.

White, K. W., and Weight, B. H. (2000). *The online teaching guide*. Boston: Allyn and Bacon.

CHAPTER 7

Exploring E-Education Applications: A Framework for Analysis

Mary Helen Fagan
Assistant Professor of Information Systems
The University of Texas at Tyler

Introduction

As computers and communications have been converging, society has been moving rapidly from the Industrial Age into the Information Age. In this transition the nature of organizations, work, and learning is changing. Hierarchical and bureaucratic organizations are looking for ways to create more flexible structures capable of rapid response to environmental changes. These changing organizations need knowledge workers who are capable of quickly assimilating large amounts of information and solving diverse and unstructured problems. These knowledge workers will have to be constantly learning new skills in order to successfully solve problems in this complex, information-based, rapidly changing work and organizational environment.

These societal shifts affect colleges and universities in a number of ways (Uys, 2002). First, many educators are working to modify their curriculum and pedagogy to help graduates function more effectively as knowledge workers in the Information Age. In addition, educational institutions are also being called on to create more flexible, innovative structures so that the organization itself can respond more effectively to its rapidly changing environment. There have been repeated calls for institutions of higher education to recognize these societal shifts and embark upon needed changes. For example, in

1989 Richard L. Nolan (Professor of Business Administration, Harvard Business School) told a group of higher education leaders:

"For organizations to be viable, productive and competitive in the information economy of the 1990s and beyond, they must undergo a basic 'transformation.'" He also asserted that, "All of you have heard the word, but you just don't get it.'" (HEIRA, 1992).

Higher education is still continuing to grapple with the need to become more adaptive and competitive as evinced by the recent monograph "New Forces and New Realities: Making the Adjustment" (SCUP, 2002).

The approach of this study is based on the assumption that much can be learned from e-commerce and e-government efforts to reengineer or transform their organizational processes. In particular, this chapter looks at the approaches that have been used to classify e-commerce and e-government information technology (IT) applications and explores their relevance to higher education. The study develops an e-education framework that analyzes applications in higher education in terms of their application category and phase. Application categories include university to student, faculty to student, university to employee, university to organization, university to university, student to student, and a foundational category, internal efficiency and effectiveness applications. Application phases include providing information, providing forms, providing transactions, and finally, supporting organizational transformation. By developing a framework for analysis based on lessons learned in e-commerce and e-government, the study can provide another way of viewing an institution's IT portfolio and for mapping future application possibilities.

The chapter is organized as follows. First, the background literature is reviewed and the methodology is described. Then an e-education framework is presented along with applications that illustrate the various categories of the framework. Possible implications of the framework are discussed next, along with an exploration of how educational organizations are working to achieve IT goals, and then conclusions are stated.

Background

In the early 1990s many articles described how organizations that needed to undergo transformation could embark on a reengineering process designed to create radical change. With the growth of business process reengineering/redesign, business leaders recognized the role IT could play in radically transforming their organizations, their relationships with customers, and their relationships with business partners. The possibility of achieving transformational outcomes in government was explored in the Clinton/Gore administration (Gore, 1997), and the vision of reengineering/reinventing government continues to this day.

In the educational arena, practitioners and researchers also looked at how reengineering concepts could be applied to improve efficiency and enable transformation. One extended report, "Reengineering: A Process for Transforming Higher Education" (Penrod, 1991), provides an in-depth examination of reengineering principles, their application to higher education, and the specific implications of reengineering for campus information technology units. And while some may believe that reengineering is now passé, others note that the concepts embodied in reengineering existed prior to its popularity and continue to have relevance to organizations and society today. For example, a recent paper describes the use of reengineering for IT-enabled organizational transformation in the government (OSD Comptroller, 2002). Furthermore, Penrod's analysis of how higher education could be reengineered remains a useful document even now for organizations wishing to embark on IT-enabled process transformation.

A number of organizations have also developed case studies that share their perspective and experience with other organizations that are traveling a similar path. For example, the Executive Strategies report developed by representatives at California State University/Los Angeles entitled "What Presidents Should Know About the Integration of Information Technology on Campus" (HEIRA, 1992) provides an excellent example of how one institution evaluated the key trends in higher education and addressed these changes within their organization. In addition, journals like *The Technology Source* [1] and publications like *The Chronicle of Higher Education* [2] also provide insight into the efforts of higher education institutions to grapple with the opportunities and challenges presented by information technology and the Information Age. This literature indicates that some organizations are successful in meeting their goals (Chalambaga and Wallet-Chalambaga, 1999; Kock and Corner, 1997). However, other institutions like California State University find, like their business counterparts, that significant organizational change can create controversy and evoke strong objections (*The Chronicle of Higher Education*, 2003).

Methodology

This study is primarily based on an action research approach (Lau, 1999). Lau has been involved in implementing IT applications to meet educational needs and, also, as a user of various educational IT applications and the customer of an Information Systems (IS) group. In addition, the author has been engaged in extended action research projects exploring local e-government applications and small business e-commerce efforts. The goal of this study was to develop a framework to help understand the implementation of IT applications in higher education. The author analyzed materials from the for-profit and nonprofit sectors that can illuminate the role of IT in e-education, and used basic classification schemes from e-commerce and e-government to analyze e-education applications. Once the framework was developed and found to apply in the author's action research endeavors in higher education, examples were sought from experience and from the practitioner and academic literature that would further illustrate the various categories of IT e-education applications.

E-Education Framework

Categories

E-commerce applications are frequently described in terms of what constitutes their primary focus or purpose. Thus, Business to Consumer (B2C) applications allow businesses to provide consumers with information on products and services, perform transactions, and follow up a sale with online service. Business to Business (B2B) applications, on the other hand, allow businesses to interact electronically with other businesses (e.g., their suppliers or business partners). In the e-government area, four areas of applications can be identified: Government to Citizen, Government to Employee, Government to Business, and Government to Government (Balutis, 2001). This study proposes that these categories of e-government applications also provide a useful way to classify IT applications in education. In the context of higher education, these categories might be described as 1) University to Student (U2S); 2) University to Employee (U2E); 3) University to Organization (U2O); and 4) University to University (U2U).

In addition, the University to Student (U2S) can be broken down further. The U2S relationship can be seen to have two main aspects: administrative and academic. Therefore, for purposes of this analysis, it is assumed that U2S applications address administrative functions, and Faculty to Student (F2S) applications address the interactions involved with teaching and learning. A new and emerging type of relationship can also be identified. In the same way that eBay allows consumers to interact directly with other consumers, various online venues are being developed that allow students to interact with other students. For purposes of this analysis, we term these applications Student-to-Student (S2S) e-education.

Representative examples of the various categories of e-education applications are provided in Table 7.1 (and are drawn from the author's exposure to these applications at various institutions and the literature). A university Web site is a U2S application, while a faculty Web site is an F2S application. U2E applications might include an online training program provided over an intranet. More and more universities are following the example of e-commerce enterprises and linking their internal systems to suppliers, and a U2O application in a university environment might be an e-procurement portal. U2U applications are interuniversity systems, and include a situation where one university in a larger state system provides information (e.g., human resource data) to a system-level IT application where it is processed. And, finally, an S2S application might include software that helps support students who participate in campus government, clubs, and other sponsored organizations to communicate with each other directly.

All these categories of e-education applications should improve the internal efficiency and effectiveness (IEE) of the organization in some significant way or they are probably not wise choices for implementation. Some studies of e-government include another category of application that has no external organization interface but is designed only to use best practices and IT to reduce costs and speed up responsiveness within the organization (Van Wert, 2002). For example, the human resource department might choose to install new software that enables them to better manage applicants,

Table 7.1 E-Education Category and Examples

	E-Education Category	Representative Examples
IEE IT & BEST PRACTICES	• University to Student (U2S)	University Web site
	• Faculty to Student (F2S)	Faculty Web site
	• University to Employee (U2E)	Training intranet application
	• University to Organization (U2O)	E-procurement portal
	• University to University (U2U)	System-level human resource application
	• Student to Student (S2S)	Student government/club community

employee training, and reporting requirements. While these types of internal university IEE IT applications are important, they are not usually visible to external constituencies, and thus are represented in Table 7.1 as "IEE IT & best practices" that support other application categories.

While these categories may help to provide a framework to understand different types of e-education applications, the classification is incomplete. One university Web site, for example, provides a U2S application that may be very different from another university's Web site in terms of the features and functions it provides. One Web site may provide very basic information only, and thus provide, in essence, an online brochure. Another Web site, however, may go beyond basic information to provide a database lookup of research papers and online transactions such as course registration.

Phases

The differences between applications within the same e-education category can be fruitfully analyzed by applying an approach used in e-commerce and e-government research. As IT applications are developed and evolve over time, these applications typically become more elaborate and complex with new features and functionality. E-commerce studies explore how various projects fit into an evolutionary stage of development. Balutis (2001) suggests the following phases can be identified in e-government development efforts: 1) Phase 1: Dissemination of information; 2) Phase 2: Provision of forms; 3) Phase 3: Ability to perform transactions; and 4) Phase 4: Government transformation (e.g., resulting in processes that cross organizational boundaries in order to provide citizens with information and "seamless service"). This study proposes that these phases of e-government application evolution also provide a useful way to classify IT applications in education. In Table 7.2, example applications

Table 7.2 E-Education Framework

	CATEGORIES					
PHASES	US2	FS2	U2E	U2O	U2U	S2S
PHASE 1: PROVIDE INFORMATION	UNIVERSITY INFO WEBSITE	FACULTY INFO WEBSITE	ONLINE HANDBOOK	ONLINE ORDERING PROCEDURES	PROVIDE INFO ABOUT UNIVERSITY SYSTEM	POST INFO ABOUT CLUBS AND GROUPS
PHASE 2: PROVIDE FORMS	LIBRARY REQUEST DOCUMENT	STUDENT INFO DOCUMENT	BOOKSTORE ORDER DOCUMENT	ORDER REQUEST DOCUMENT	BENEFITS ENROLLMENT DOCUMENT	STUDENT CLUB SIGN-UP DOCUMENT
PHASE 3: PERFORM TRANSACTIONS	ONLINE LIBRARY REQUEST FORM	ONLINE GRADE VIEWING	CHANGE BENEFITS ONLINE	ELECTRONIC PRODUCT ORDERING	INTER-UNIVERSITY PROCESSES	ONLINE RESUME SEARCH
PHASE 4: TRANSFORM ORGANIZATION	"CLICK AND MORTAR" AND VIRTUAL UNIVERSITIES					

are shown for the phases and categories of the e-education framework.

For example, in University-to-Student (U2S) applications a Phase 1 Web site would only provide information and probably a way to interact via an e-mail hyperlink. A Phase 2 U2S Web site might provide copies of documents that could be downloaded and then mailed, faxed, or perhaps attached to an e-mail for return to the appropriate department. Thus, a library might provide an online copy of their interlibrary loan request document as a U2S application. With Phase 3 development, a U2S Web site would provide support for transactions of various kinds. For example, instead of a document to be sent back via e-mail, a library might provide an online form that, when filled out, initiates an interlibrary loan request automatically. Phase 3 U2S applications might involve financial transactions, such as bill payment, or support database queries that build a response page dynamically. All these applications improve efficiency and effectiveness, but they may not achieve Phase 4 levels of educational organization transformation.

In Phase 4, e-education would support "seamless service" so that users would find applications organized around the events that interest them and not around the departments that make up the organization. Phase 4 IT applications across key categories of the e-education framework would support both "click and mortar" and virtual universities. "Click and mortar" institutions would combine the best of online and physical education in a seamless manner. It is envisioned that success in this objective would require the transformation of most traditional institutions of higher education to provide a robust campuswide information system that is not bounded by geography. The goal of Phase 4 development is the vision that has enlivened e-government supporters, and this vision has been furthered by those in education who support the possibilities inherent in e-learning. But, as a whole, a university might not view their entire IT applications portfolio, administrative as well as academic, as an integrated toolset designed to serve their customers in a seamless, unified way. This view underlies the e-education framework that is presented here.

In the e-commerce environment, various application software packages are available to meet the requirements of these different categories shown in Table 7.1 and described in Table 7.2. In Figure 7.1, typical applications used in the business environment are mapped to the various application categories in the e-education framework. An organization might use this type of approach to begin to analyze how they are meeting the various needs outlined in this paper's e-education framework. For example, business-to-customer application needs are frequently met in the business environment by what are called Customer Relationship Management Systems. In higher education, many organizations have pushed to develop strategic enrollment systems that identify, track, and serve potential students (U2S). Similarly, the need to support internal efficiency and effectiveness in various functional areas is frequently supported by what are called Enterprise Systems in the business environment. A number of educational institutions have worked to implement systems from vendors such as PeopleSoft and Oracle to support these functions in their environment (IEE) (EDUCAUSE, 2000). These enterprise systems also support the information and decision-making needs of employees (U2E). Inter-organizational systems support relationships with a variety of business partners, and in the educational environment these systems support things such as electronic transcript exchange between universities (U2U) and financial information exchange with government entities (U2O) (Luker, 2002). In a similar way, supply chain management systems in business and in higher education serve to link purchasing agents and users with qualified suppliers to make the procurement process more efficient (U2O). Finally, in higher education all of these various systems exist to support an institution's primary mission—the learning process. In this area, various course management software applications are in use (F2S and S2S).

Many educational institutions are working to move from Phase 1 to higher-level phases in many of these application categories. Unfortunately, higher education organizations face the same challenges encountered by their business and government counterparts: too frequently these various applications are not integrated and a common infrastructure is not in place to support these diverse application initiatives effectively.

Discussion

Many educational institutions face severe challenges in planning strategically for IT, implementing effectively, and supporting users. These challenges face all IT specialists in organizations facing a rapidly changing IT landscape. However, in a time of tight budgets and continued high expectations, IT departments in higher education may find themselves asked to do more with fewer resources (Yole, 1996 and Martin, 2003). Even Phase 1 applications like a U2S Web site can be fraught with difficulty. How can IT departments be expected to work toward Phase 2 and 3 applications, and the highest level Phase 4 organizational transformation, when providing Phase 1 application development and user-support consumes their staff and financial resources?

With so many potential categories of applications, the key at most institutions has to revolve around the IT strategic planning process and the presence of a strong chief information officer (CIO) (Penrod, 2003). However, based on a small sample of institutions familiar to

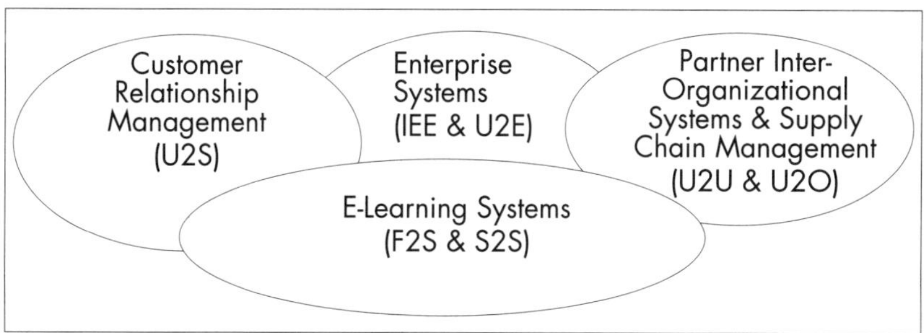

Figure 7.1 E-Education System

the author, and based on a review of some of the literature, this is often a challenging goal to achieve. In one institution, the administrative and academic departments reported to different executive officers, and there was not, until recently, any high-level strategic IT planning process in place. Furthermore, an outstanding CIO commands an outstanding salary, and in one institution that tried to recruit a CIO who would function at a dean's level and be responsible for all administrative, academic, and library computing, the institution hired and lost three CIOs in as many years. Evidence of the need for a university administrator's direction is evinced by the fact that one of the best-selling publications of the Society for College and University Planning is a book on how to transform higher education to meet the challenges (and opportunities) of the Information Age (Dolence, 1995). Many IT administrators agree that the process starts with a CIO who can work with others to develop a shared vision of IT while managing the daily IT operations processes (Penrod, 2003).

When the IT organization is functioning optimally, then slack resources can be made available to help move toward higher phases of IT application. For example, recognizing the need for users to have "seamless service" organized around their life events and needs and not organization structure, some universities have developed separate Web sites to meet the needs of prospective students only [3]. When developing a virtual university, these processes are designed "from a blank slate" making it feasible to create new seamless service models that provide all aspects of administration and academics in a user-friendly way. The challenge may be more difficult when a university or universities in a state system are looking to move from a "bricks and mortar" to a "clicks and mortar" educational model. For example, it's not uncommon that when multiple campuses decide to share online courses or programs, each campus has to deal with registration processes that were developed specifically for that campus. Sometimes those processes involve paper forms required by one of the offices to be submitted, even though it's an online registration process. Other researchers have documented the many pedagogical and political challenges associated with changing from a physical to a more virtual teaching and learning environment, and how the support processes are affected (Chizmar and Williams, 1998). Virtual design will be streamlined and improved over time, but it illustrates the challenges that face universities as they move into new areas and are faced with the prospect of transforming how they have always done things within their own organization to meet new needs.

Conclusion

Some academics are uncomfortable with applying models from industry and government to education. Academics, on the other hand, may be perceived as clinging to the ivory tower, hoping that the wave of IT-enabled transformation that is changing many industries will pass by their educational establishment. Perhaps, as one analysis points out, "a significant part of the difficulty of thinking about reengineering in higher education arises from the absence of clear analogs between industry and colleges and universities" (Stahlke and Nyce, 1996). This chapter applies frameworks from industry and government to education, and thus works to help develop useful analogs for analysis by looking at processes, interdepartment and intercampus interaction, and software. This e-education framework can provide a useful way of thinking about IT applications in higher education in terms of their application category and phase of development. Furthermore, the framework provides a way of looking at the IT applications portfolio in education that can help map similar educational functions to their corresponding functionality in business applications (e.g., strategic enrollment management to customer relationship management). With strong CIO leadership, a robust strategic planning process, and effective implementation practices, many educational institutions can achieve the benefits of IT touted by industry, and avoid some of the pitfalls as they move toward the goal of seamless customer service and e-education delivery.

Endnotes

1. Available at http://ts.mivu.org/default.asp
2. Available at http://chronicle.com
3. Examples of such schools are http://www.smu.edu/audience/prospectivestudents and http://www.virginia.edu/ofstud.html

References

Balutis, A. P. (2001). "E-government 2001, Part I: Understanding the Challenge and Evolving Strategies," *The Public Manager*, Spring, Vol. 30, No. 1: 33–37.

Chalambaga, M. S., and Wallet-Chalambaga, K. A. (1999). "The Technology Caterpillar or Productivity Butterfly? A Technological Metamorphosis," *Campus-Wide Information Systems*, Vol. 16, No. 5: 171–175.

Chizmar, J. F., and Williams, D. B. (1998). "Internet Delivery of Instruction: Issues of Best Teaching Practice, Administrative Hurdles, and Old-Fashioned Politics," *Campus-Wide Information Systems*, Vol. 15, No. 5: 164–173.

Chronicle of Higher Education (2003). "Giant Cal State Computing Project Leaves Professors and Students Asking, Why?: Administrators see Efficiencies, but Academics Fear Loss of Control," *The Chronicle of Higher Education*, January 17, 2003. Available from http://chronicle.com/free/v49/i19/19a02701.htm

Dolance, M. G., and Norris, D. M. (1995). *Transforming higher education: A vision for learning in the 21st century*. Ann Arbor, MI: Society for College and University Planning.

EDUCAUSE (2000). "Administrative Information Systems," *EDUCAUSE Review*, January/February: 56N58. Available from http://www.educause.edu/pub/er/erm00/pp056059.pdf

Gore, A. (1997). "Introduction" in the Report of the National Performance Review and the Government Information Technology Services Board, Access America. Available from http://govinfo.library.unt.edu/accessamerica/docs/intro.html

Kock, N. F., and Corner, J. L. (1997). "Improving University Processes through Computer-Mediated Process Redesign Groups," *Campus-Wide Information Systems*, Vol. 14, No. 1: 13–23.

Lau, F. (1999). "Toward a Framework for Action Research in Information Systems Studies," *Information Technology & People*, Vol. 12, No. 2: 148–175.

Luker, M. A. (2002). "A Bridge for Trusted Electronic Communications in Higher Education and the Government," *EDUCAUSE Review*, January/February: 40–49. Available http://www.educause.edu/ir/library/pdf/erm0203.pdf

Martin, M. (2003). "Top IT Issue: Doing More With Less," *NewsFactor Top Tech News Online*, June 30, 2003. Available from http://www.newsfactor.com/story.xhtml?story_id=218195

OSD Comptroller (2002). *Reengineering: A Radical Approach to Business Process Design,* U.S. Department of Defense. Available from http://www.dod.mil/comptroller/icenter/learn/reeng.htm

Penrod, J. I. (2003). "Creating a Realistic IT Vision: The Roles and Responsibilities of a Chief Information Officer," *The Technology Source,* March/April. Available from http://ts.mivu.org/default.asp?show=article&id=1030

Penrod, J. I., and Harbor, A. F. (1998). "Building a Client-Focused IT Organization," *Campus-Wide Information Systems,* Vol. 15, No. 3: 91–102.

Penrod, J. I., and Dolence, M. G. (1991). *Reengineering: A Process for Transforming Higher Education,* PUB3009, CAUSE. Available from http://www.educause.edu/ir/library/pdf/PUB3009.pdf

SCUP (2002). *New Forces and New Realities: Making the Adjustment.* The Society for College and University Planning, National Planning Roundtable Monograph. Available http://www.scup.org/nfr/

Stahlke, H. F. W., and Nyce, J. M. (1996). "Reengineering Higher Education: Reinventing Teaching and Learning," *CAUSE/EFFECT,* Vol. 19, No. 4: 44–51. Available http://www.educause.edu/ir/library/html/cem9649.html

Uys, P. (2002). "Networked Educational Management: Transforming Educational Management in a Networked Institute," *Campus-Wide Information Systems,* Vol. 19, No. 5: 175–181.

Van Wert, J. M. (2002). "E-Government and Performance: A Citizen-Centered Imperative," *The Public Manager,* Summer: 16–20.

Yole, J. M. (1996). "Information Technology Support Service: Crisis or Opportunity," *Campus-Wide Information Systems,* Vol. 13, No. 4: 14–23.

Part 2

Best Practices in Administrative Operations

Chapters in this section deal with projects that provide new services or substantially augment existing services yielding more effective and efficient operations.

One of the newest functions of college administrative systems is workflow, a process that can link together multiple operations formerly done on paper and track them on the system. For example, a payroll request may need to be originated in a department, then routed to the budget office for its approval, to a supervisor for her approval, and finally to a vice-president. Workflow allows this process to be done electronically, tracking where the request is in the queue and providing feedback to the originator. The workflow process is likely to revolutionize administrative operations because of the ability to duplicate paper processes and provide feedback. Examples included here are the requisition process and the paperless Financial Aid office.

There are two categories of workflow applications. One we have just described, the other is "notification workflow," as in, "Let me know when something happens" (formerly done with carbon copy paper, i.e., tell me when a student withdraws, tell me when a student falls below full-time status, etc.). Here are some additional examples:

Process workflows	*Notification workflows*
Grade entry	Tell me when my budget is 90 percent spent

Transfer funds between accounts	E-mail vice-president when donation over a certain amount is entered
New system account requests	E-mail alumni chair upon death of an alum
Student check-in	

An online registration conversion from touch-tone registration is described and the University of Dayton describes its Web site personalization project that uses administrative data to populate Web fields, giving the student "ownership" of her page and information.

Finally, we offer a best practices discussion of data warehousing as a means to provide more efficient information gathering from relational databases. If you're not a techie, this means grouping logical information for reporting purposes instead of spreading it out all over the system. Relational databases, for example, may track names in one file, addresses in another, phone numbers in yet another, etc. So, providing address labels may require access to six tables; grade reports might call for access to 50 or more. Data warehousing makes it easier for the nontechie to access information and often decreases the processing time on administrative systems because reporting can be done from a separate database instead of the main database that all offices are using for data entry and retrieval.

CHAPTER 8

HR Quick Requisition Process

Elaine Peters
Employment Manager, Human Resources,
and Jane Gao, Programmer/Analyst,
Administrative Computing Services
University of California, Irvine

UC Irvine

Since its founding in 1965, the University of California, Irvine (UCI) has combined the strengths of a major research university with the bounty of an incomparable Southern California location. In fewer than four decades, UCI has become internationally recognized for efforts that are improving lives through research and discovery, providing excellence in scholarship and teaching, and engaging and enriching the community.

The Quick Requisition

The application we developed is called the Quick Requisition. The goal of this project was to streamline and automate the staff employment requisition process for hiring managers and employment recruiters. By reducing and eliminating the paper-driven recruitment process, we anticipated significant improvements in the response time to begin the recruitment process and increased satisfaction with the overall process for hiring managers. The many constraints of the existing process included the limitation that job requisitions for recruitment could only be posted once a week on the Human Resources Employment Web site. Because of this, hiring managers experienced delays in beginning the recruitment process and in receiving the resumes of qualified job candidates.

Human resources also conducted a campuswide employment survey that was distributed to high-volume users of the recruitment process. The survey included questions regarding the importance of the requisition and recruitment process flow, ease of use, selection and quality of applicants. The major concern identified in the results of the survey was the timeliness of the recruitment process. Specifically, users felt it took too long to post a job and get the recruitment started—there was a 10-day waiting period. Hiring managers were concerned that initiating a recruitment process was not timely.

To gain additional feedback, human resources invited key campus constituents to participate in a recruitment process focus group. The focus group set process priorities, evaluated ideas for redesign, and gave recommendations for change. Their recommendations included an easier process, the use of technology to streamline the requisition recruitment process, and a faster turnaround time to receive and review applicant resumes.

A project team was convened, which included members of the human resources employment staff and members of the campus administrative computing services department. The team's goal was to develop a technology solution for the requisition recruitment process. Quick Requisition is the name of the human resources/technology solution that was used to streamline and automate the requisition posting process. Quick Requisition allows hiring departments to enter requisitions electronically for forwarding electronically to the campus budget office (if needed) for approval, or directly to human resources (if this is a self-funded department). The new process eliminates the need to submit a paper requisition and significantly streamlines the requisition approval process for hiring departments and for human resources employment staff. The Quick Requisition data is automatically imported into the Web-based employment system, thereby eliminating the need for human resources employment staff to manually enter the data.

The implementation of Quick Requisition demonstrated significant benefits to the university. The recruitment cycle time has been reduced from 10 weeks to 6 weeks. UCI has set the standard for its sister campuses and received recognition for the implementation of Quick Requisition.

Additionally, hiring departments have benefited from Quick Requisition since the job descriptions and requisitions are entered into the Quick Requisition database, and thus are available to be retrieved, modified, and used for future recruiting needs. The database of job descriptions provides a valuable tool for hiring managers and helps to reduce their workload when recruiting for a position.

The human resources employment staff has benefited from the innovation and has been able to provide much more of a partnership and strategic role with hiring managers. Eliminating the need for data entry and processing of requisitions has given them the opportunity to appropriately screen applicant resumes and work with hiring departments on recruitment strategies, interviews, and employment offer negotiations.

Human resources conducted training classes for users of Quick Requisition and offered an online training guide. An additional goal of the project was to make the process as easy as possible for users, with a training time of 30 minutes or less. Users can be self-taught using the training guide.

The project has been very successful due to the involvement of campus users and the human resources employment staff in the design, development, and implementation of the project. Involving the appropriate individuals and campus users promoted acceptance and willingness to change. The project was implemented in a team environment, which increased ownership of the process from start until completion.

Advice for others implementing a similar project is to get those individuals who will use the process involved early in the design stages. This was a key to the success of our project. Additionally, understanding the user's needs and concerns is key to implementing changes. Creating a mechanism for feedback before, during, and after the process also helps ensure buy-in and satisfaction from those using the application.

Quick Requisition Application Structure

Figures 8.1 and 8.2 demonstrate the simplicity of the Quick Requisition system.

Who developed Quick Requisition?

Quick Requisition was developed by Jane Gao, Technical Project Leader in UCI's Administrative Computing Services (ADCOM).

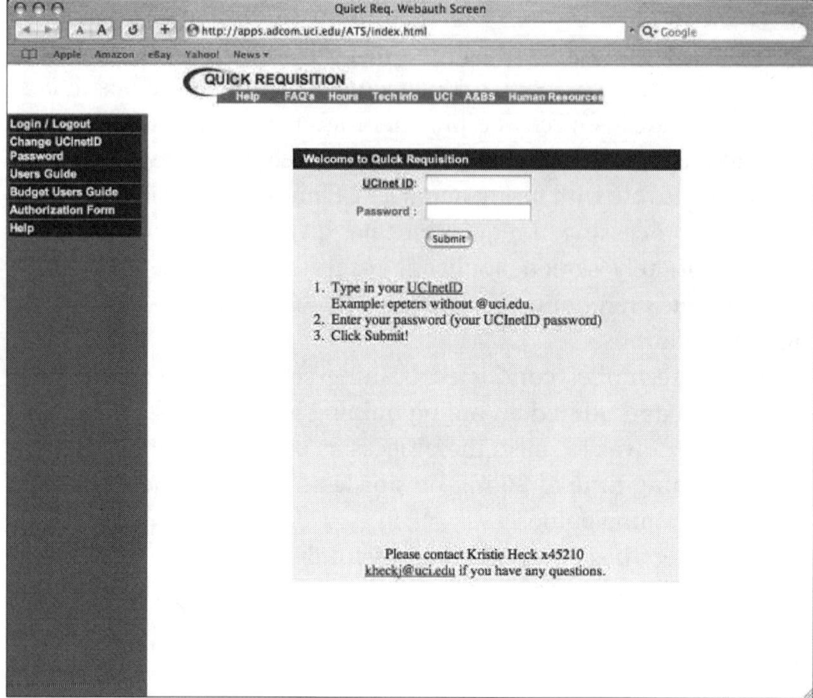

Figure 8.1 Quick Requisition 1

How was the application developed?

Quick Requisition is designed to communicate with the UCI Employment system to perform real-time job posting to UCI Web pages. It streamlines the whole job requisition process including job request, approval, and task routing processes.

How Quick Requisition Works

Quick Requisition is an *n*-tiered, Web-based client-server application. It runs across internetworking with multiple platforms and different browsers.

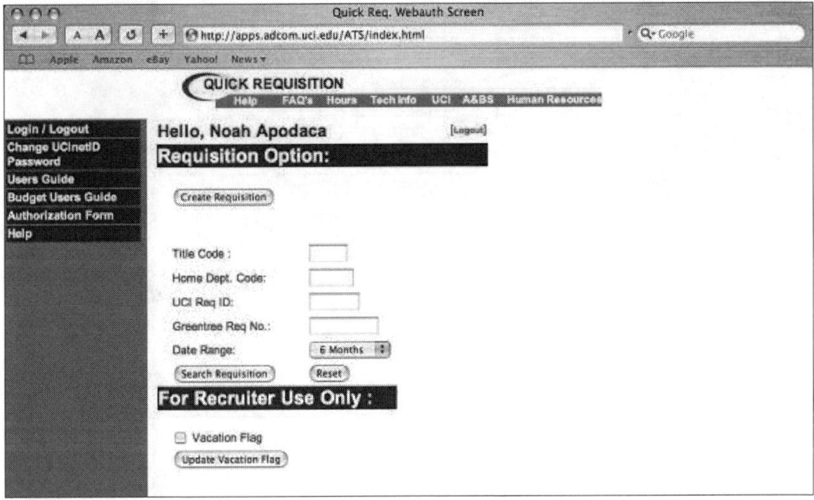

Figure 8.2 Quick Requisition 2

- Its presentation tier is a Web-based GUI, which is built on JSP, HTML, DHTML, and XML.
- Its business logic tier is developed in JAVA and built on Tomcat/Apache Web server. Plus, Quick Requisition is utilized with third party application iGreentree by using XML technology.
- Its data access tier is funneled access to its data store resided in MSSQL server and UCI DataWareHouse (DWH), which is stored in Sybase server.

Therefore, by using component-based architecture, Quick Requisition possesses the flexibility for enhancement upgrade and business rule changes. This application uses cutting edge technologies including Java, JSP, XML, DHTML, MS SQL server, etc.

Figures 8.3 and 8.4 demonstrate the technical and functional operation of the Quick Requisition process.

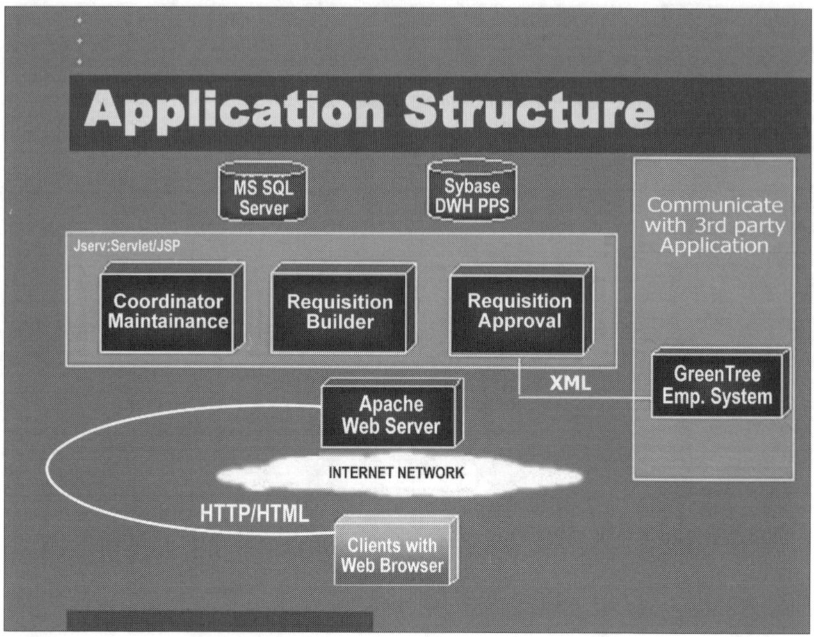

Figure 8.3 Quick Requisition Application Structure

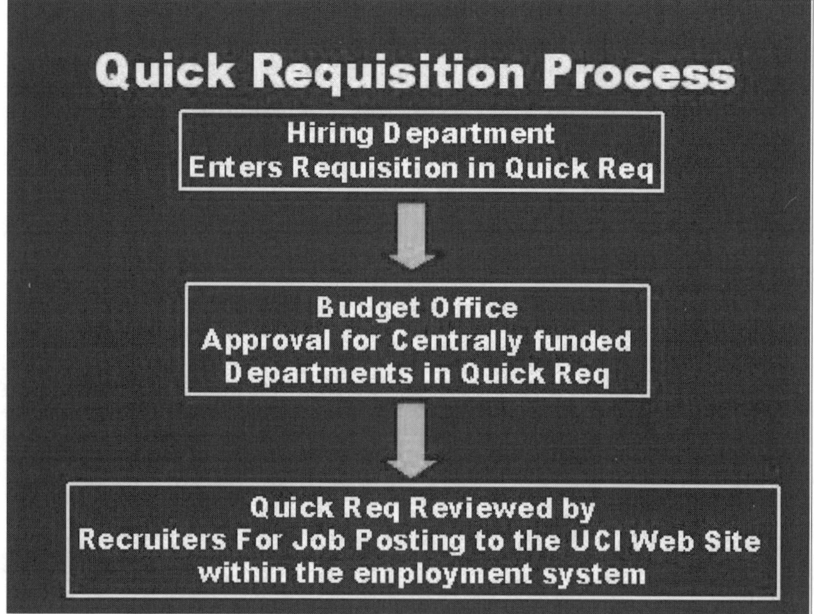

Figure 8.4 How Quick Requisition Works

Conclusion

In conclusion, Quick Requisition has greatly improved the cycle time for the UCI recruitment process. This solution has improved our customer service and has demonstrated Human Resources' ability to partner with hiring departments to develop innovative solutions to the changing HR function.

CHAPTER 9

The Paperless Financial Aid Office

Nancy Sinsabaugh
Consultant and Former Interim Director of Student Finance
University of Minnesota

With a budget of $1.9 billion and annual federal research expenditures of $334 million, the University of Minnesota (UofMN) has four campuses: the Twin Cities (47,273 students); Duluth (9,385 students); Crookston (2,070 students); and Morris (1,828 students).

In July 2001 the University of Minnesota, with its four campuses and more than 60,000 students, inaugurated its "Paperless Financial Aid Office" initiative, which allows for students to apply for, process, and receive more than $200 million annually in federal and institutional aid without touching a single piece of paper.

One of the nation's most prestigious public research universities, the University of Minnesota prides itself on its Web culture and state-of-the-art student service delivery. In the spring of 2001, then President Mark Yudof announced that the University of Minnesota would become a paperless university and that e-mail would become the official means of communication between the university and its students.

To meet the president's challenge, the University of Minnesota's Office of Student Finance (combining financial aid and bursar functions) sought a way to improve student service by using state-of-the-art technology tools. With PeopleSoft Student Administration System software already in place, financial aid functional managers brainstormed with an in-house Web-development team to come up with the project design (Figure 9.1). The project took seventeen months from the time of inception to time of completion and coincided with the Department of Education's e-signature initiative for Stafford Loans.

Scope

Figure 9.1 illustrates the Paperless Financial Aid Office. The players include students, University of Minnesota staff, and the U.S. Department of Education (ED). Prospective students apply online to the UofMN. Using ED's online Free Application for Federal Student Aid (FAFSA), prospective and returning students apply for federal, state, and institutional financial aid. An ED contractor processes the application and electronically sends a data file to the UofMN with eligibility and other data for each prospective and returning student. At the UofMN, admissions, registration, and eligibility information, along with the UofMN budget projections, provide the basis for student aid packaging performed in PeopleSoft. Once the aid is packaged and Financial Aid Award Notices (FAANs) prepared, the student is sent an e-mail notification that his FAAN is available on the Office of Student Finance Web site. Students locate the Web site, enter their UofMN secure ID, and view their FAANs.

Students have the opportunity online to accept grants and scholarships, accept or reject loans, and, in some cases, reduce loan amounts. Links are provided to determine each loan, grant, or scholarship for which the student is eligible. Once students have completed these transactions, they are asked to confirm their intention to enroll for the next two semesters and to credit their financial aid funds.

Once all transactions are completed, the Web site reviews the student's choices before prompting the student to finalize her decisions. The student can then review the accepted aid listed on the Web site.

The University of Minnesota is a Direct Lending school and sends loan origination data electronically to ED's Loan Origination Center (LOC) for each Stafford Loan accepted. If the student has not yet signed a Master Promissory Note, the LOC notifies the UofMN, which, in turn, sends the student an e-mail with links to ED's Direct Loan Web site so the student can sign the loan electronically.

Once the Master Promissory Note has been signed, the LOC informs the UofMN that funds can be disbursed, as early as 10 days before the beginning of the semester. When funds are disbursed to the student's account, an e-mail is sent to the student notifying her of the disbursement. If the student has signed up for direct deposit, any credit balance will be sent to the student's bank account.

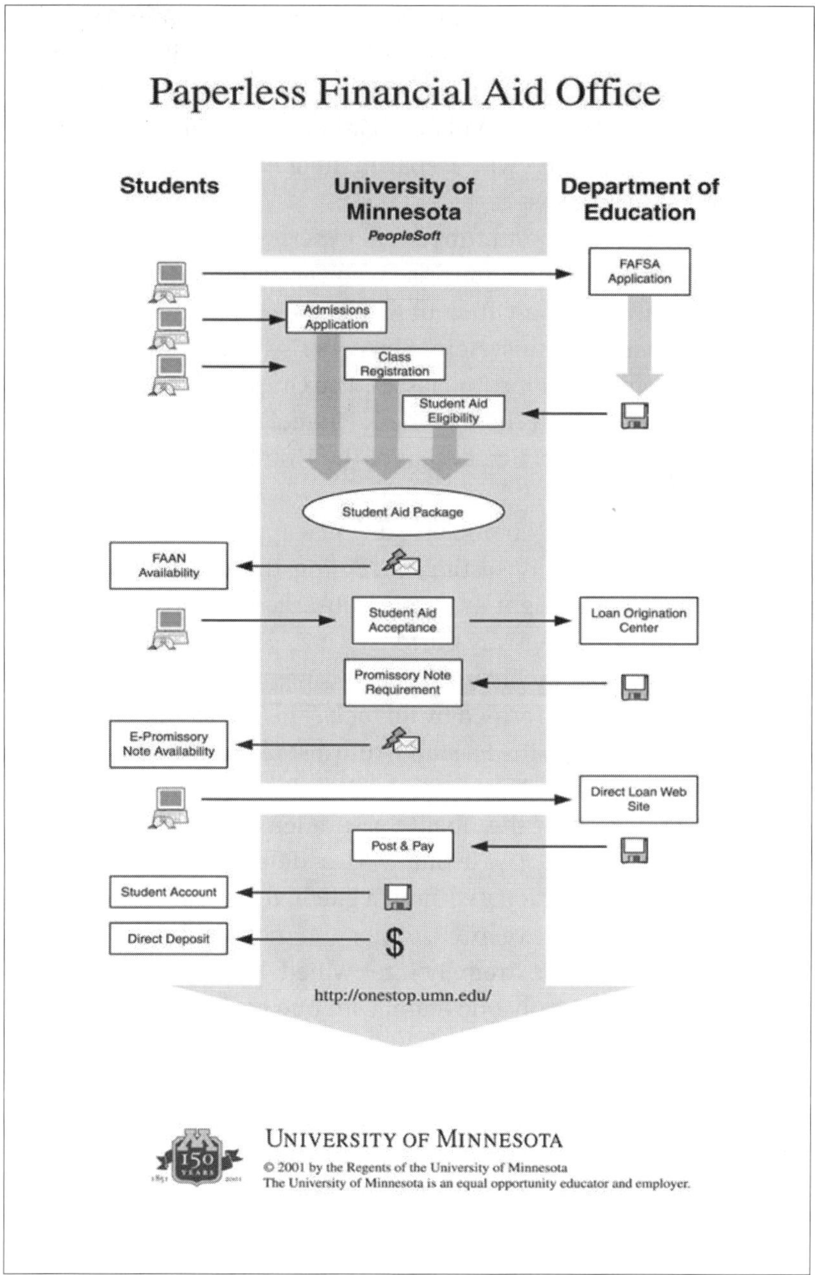

Figure 9.1 Paperless Financial Aid Office

The Paperless Financial Aid Office innovations include: 1) e-mail notification that a student's financial aid notice is available; 2) Web-based FAANs; 3) the ability to accept or reject aid and reduce loan amounts via the Web; 4) e-mail notifications that student loans need e-signatures; and 5) links with Department of Education's e-signature process for Direct Loans.

University technical and functional experts created the Paperless Financial Aid Office. The Enterprise Web Development team worked in conjunction with the Office of Student Finance to define, code, test, and implement the system. Since 1997, UofMN students have been able to register online for classes. The Graphical User Interface's (GUI) "look and feel" of the Paperless Financial Aid Office extended the already proven effective design of the UofMN's student registration system.

The entire Paperless Financial Aid Office application was submitted to rigorous usability testing, including the execution of three detailed scenarios by eight evaluators observed interacting with the prototype through a one-way mirror.

The analysis was facilitated by a business analyst on the Web group, and actually performed by financial aid (FA) staff. While development was underway, the FA staff wrote test plans, which were coordinated by the test coordinator on the Web development team. Upon successful execution of the quality assurance plan, the system was moved to production. The result was a defect-free product fully implemented on the first try without a glitch, technical or functional.

The relationship between customer (financial aid) and supplier (Web development) is extremely intertwined. While the project was underway, there was truly one team, with one goal in mind. The Web development project manager managed scope and progress tightly. Project status was reported regularly to the business and technical sponsors, Nancy Sinsabaugh and Kari Branjord. A sense of equality pervaded the project team because each member brought a specific skill-set and particular knowledge to the table.

Project Team

Office of Student Finance: Nancy Sinsabaugh, Megan Kamrath, Ken Kiehm, Judy Swanson

Office of Information Technology: Kari Branjord, Jake Gage, Gretchen Haas, Jim Hall, Allison Jacobsen, Chris Rigsby, Paul Rubenis, Scott Ruud, Royce Shin, Raji Srinivasan, Bruce Stone

Who Benefited and How?

The benefits of the Paperless Financial Aid Office were numerous and surprising. Students benefited from quicker processing time. The project cost $245,000 budget details are shown in Table 9.1. Staff could focus all their attention on students rather than on pushing paper. Technical staff morale improved because they truly enjoy working on projects that improve student services. With such a successful result, functional and technical staff are proud of their time well spent.

Figures 9.2 and 9.3 demonstrate the flow of information through the Financial Aid office before and afer the project was implemented.

Table 9.1 Web Development Costs

Phase One:		
Project Duration: 4 months	Time	Compensation
Project Manager	100%	$40,000
2 Java Programmers	100%	$80,000
Design and Usability	100%	$40,000
Business Analysis	50%	$20,000
Production Preparation	50%	$20,000
Total		$200,000
Phase Two:		
Project Duration: 2 months		
Project Manager	100%	$20,000
2 Java Programmers	100%	$20,000
Production Preparation	25%	$5,000
Total		$45,000

Note: 1. These numbers include salary and fringe. 2. The average cost of an Enterprise Web Development staff member is $120,000 per year.

Before the inauguration of the Paperless Financial Aid office, processing financial aid from the time the Financial Aid Award Notice was sent to the student to the time aid was ready to be disbursed took an average of six weeks. After implementation, the average time was four days.

The success of the Paperless Financial Aid Office was immediately obvious. Financial aid information and transaction capability is now readily available 22 hours a day, seven days a week, from anywhere in the world. Speed of aid delivery, from the time the FAAN is available to the date of aid disbursement has improved from six weeks (Figure 9.2) to four days (Figure 9.3). Processing problems that were eliminated include returned mail, receipt of forms with incorrect information, handling delays caused by 500,000 pieces of paper, and long lines at the UofMN Student Service Center. Students' feedback indicated that students enjoy transacting university business at 2 A.M. Staff morale improved because staff spent time working with students rather than pushing paper. With less overtime and weekend work, staff members can now enjoy Minnesota's August weather. The Office of Student Finance saves $80,000 a year in printing, mailing, overtime pay, and temporary help, providing for a three-year payback of the initial $245,000 technology investment.

Meanwhile, the boxes that held the half million pieces of paper no longer clog the corridors of the Office of Student Finance (Table 9.2).

The UofMN culture of using the Web whenever possible for transactions involving students contributed to this hugely successful implementation. First, a proven, effective, centralized technical help desk process was in place to assist users with technical questions. Second, e-mail had already been proclaimed an official means of communication between the institution and the student. A thorough publicity campaign, including advertisements in the student newspaper, discussion during freshman orientation, e-mail, and posters alerted students to this development prior to the implementation of the FA system. Third, online registration had been in place for several years at the University of Minnesota, so all students were accustomed to the login screens and process. Fourth, security issues had been addressed consistently and frequently, resulting in predictable system behavior from the student perspective. (For example, students were familiar with SSL encryption because it is consistently employed in the self-service Web systems.) Finally, other key and complex processes had been Web-enabled prior to the

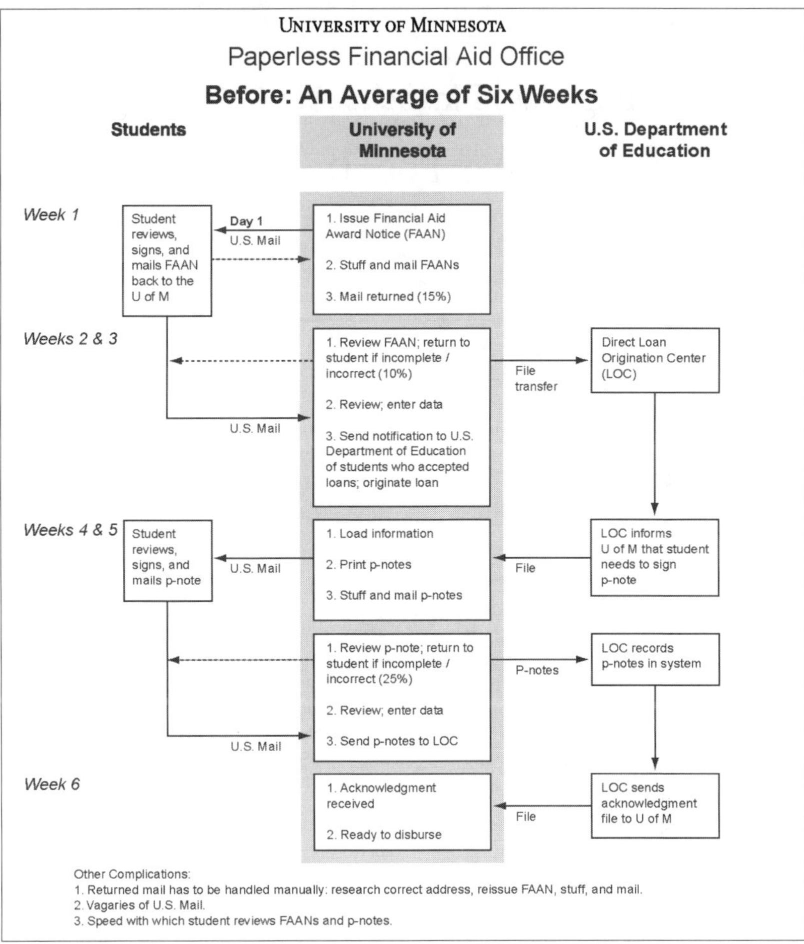

Figure 9.2 The Paperless Financial Aid Office Before Implementation

implementation of the Paperless Financial Aid Office. Registration and the associated decision support systems, housing application and reapplication, admissions applications, etc., were familiar systems to current students.

This concept is applicable to any school with Web capability or an integrated student services system. We have demonstrated how it works at state, regional, and national conferences. Articles about the Paperless Financial Aid Office have appeared in *The Chronicle of*

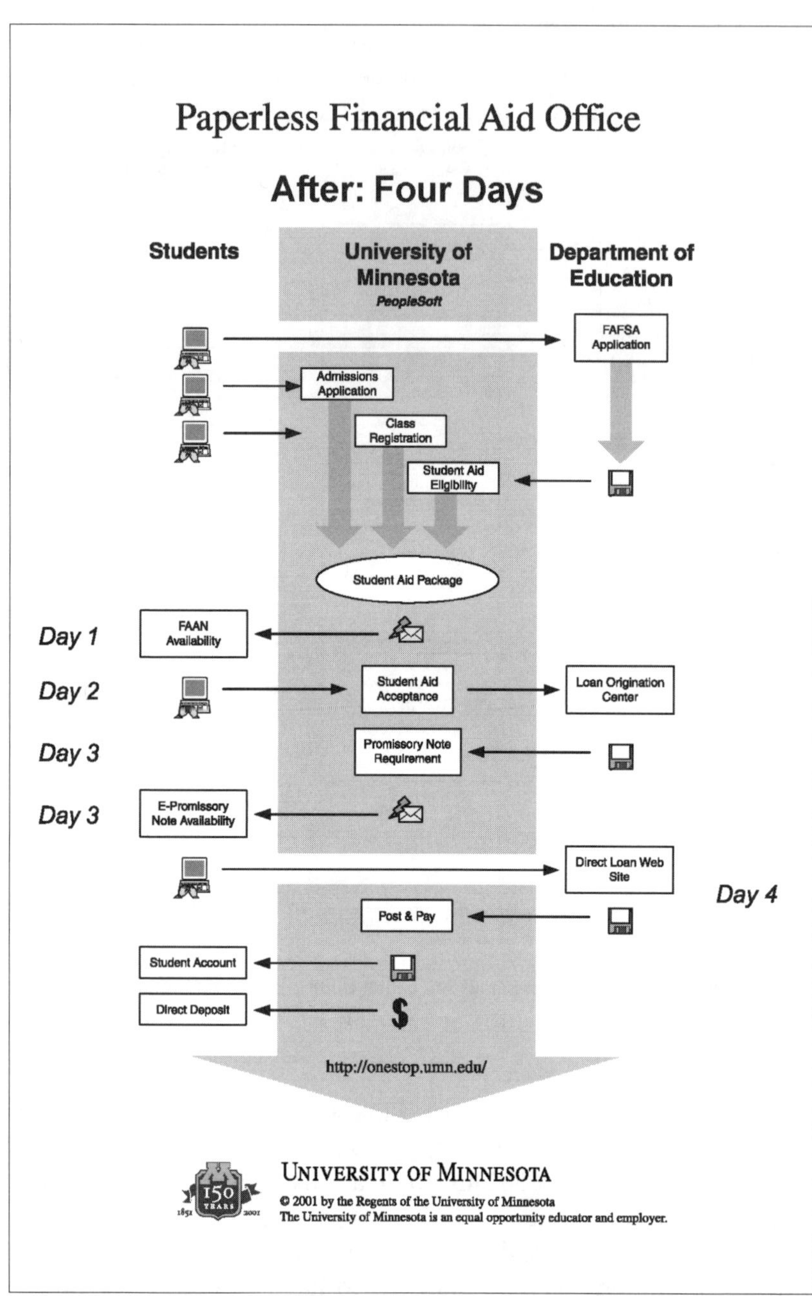

Figure 9.3 The Paperless Financial Aid Office After Implementation

Table 9.2 Paperless Financial Aid Office Savings

Paper eliminated:

33,000	Financial Aid Award Notices
33,000	Envelopes
	Remailed because of wrong addresses (15%):
4,950	FAANs
4,950	Envelopes
3,300	Return of incomplete FAANS (illegible signatures, no signatures, etc.) (10%):
3,300	Envelopes
11,550	Revised Award Notices (i.e., credit hour changes, additional aid) (35%):
11,550	Envelopes
344,000	Promissory notes (8 copies/loan) – 43,000/year x 8
43,000	Envelopes
43,000	Disclosure forms
535,600	

Cost reductions:

Temporary Help	$26,602.96
Overtime Cost	4,268.62
FAAN Printing Cost	14,451.60
FAAN (including revised FAANs) Mailing Cost	25,504.06
Promissory Notes Printing Cost	2,674.71
Promissory Notes Mailing Cost	5,691.39
All Other Loans Printing Cost	733.02
All Other Loans Mailing Cost	1,067.60
Total	$80,993.96

Higher Education, *NACUBO Business Officer*, *Chicago Tribune*, and various St. Paul and Minneapolis newspapers.

Technical Architecture

In addition to the applicable business model, several technical components provide an excellent example for other higher education institutions. For a diagram of the technical components, see Figure 9.4.

In the department of the technical architecture for the paperless Financial Aid offices we set four goals:

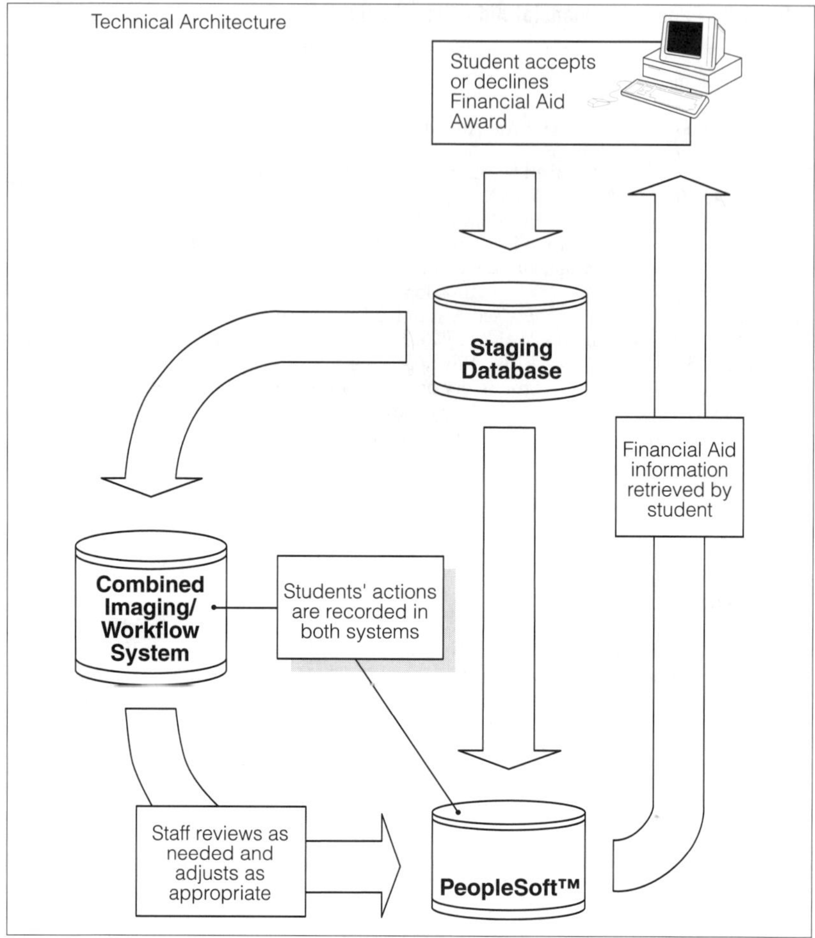

Figure 9.4 The Paperless Financial Aid Office Technical Architecture

a) First, we leverage existing, proven user-interface designs. Students respond better to the comfortable extensions of functionality they are accustomed to than to the implementation of brand new buttons, boxes, and vocabulary. Our model has the UofMN online registration system, which had already been in place for several years

b) Because of the inherent complexity in financial aid and calculations and the frequency with which financial aid regulations change, a second goal was to leave the business logic in the foundational system, with only navigational logic in the Web front end. Nowhere in the paperless Financial Aid offer does the logic on the Web replicate or attempt to replace the regulatory logic that rightfully exists in the back end system, PeopleSoft.

c) We also utilized a Usability Evaluation process before coding began. With a possible user-base of 33,000 individuals, the institution could not afford to create a product that would be confusing to the user.

d) Finally, we needed to be able to easily adapt to future increases in demand. Housing the Web and application servers on Intel Linux servers is a reliable, stable, cost-effective method of achieving this scalability. That is, if we find we need additional capacity, it will cost less than $5,000 to increase throughput by another 100 concurrent users.

The success of the Paperless Financial Aid office has far exceeded everyone's expectations. During its inaugural season, 87 percent of financial aid eligible students used the Web to transact their aid. Paper was reduced to a bare minimum. To our surprise, staff morale improved significantly; employees would rather work with students on individual financial aid challenges than push paper. We were honored that the Paperless Financial Aid Office was awarded the 2002 Educause Award for Excellence in Administration and Information Systems. Finally, and perhaps most importantly, we proved that functional and technical staff at the University of Minnesota had learned valuable lessons during our PeopleSoft Student Administration and Human Resources ERP implementation: that by working together as a team, we could achieve major service improvements which would never be possible without teamwork and the opportunities that information technology provides.

CHAPTER 10

Online Registration

Fred Dear
Associate Registrar
University of Southern California

The University of Southern California is a private four-year institution with master's and doctoral programs. Bachelor degrees are offered in 77 undergraduate majors and master's, doctoral, and professional degrees in 139 areas of study. Enrollment is 30,700 and the academic calendar is semester. Located near the heart of Los Angeles, USC is a major private research university and a member of the Association of American Universities.

While the present TouchTone system (offered at USC since 1989) allows students to register with maximum convenience and effectively mirrors all edits and processes of the online enrollment system, the system is limited in the amount of other pertinent information that is provided to students. As the new Web registration system was in the design stages, it was deemed essential that a new system contain the following features:

- Curriculum information with links to course descriptions and syllabi
- Schedule information with links to schedule of classes and such pertinent information as day, time, location, instructor, seats available.
- Degree information with a link to degree audit, courses completed/needed and major/minor requirements

Figure 10.1 shows the course selection screen in USC's online registration system.

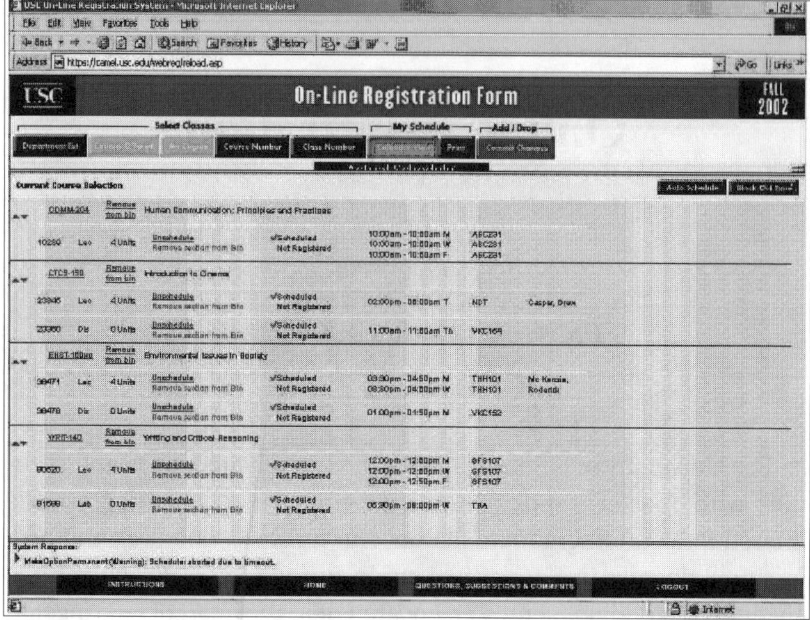

Figure 10.1 Final Course Selection

An essential consideration for a new system was that it must not only duplicate the advantages of the present TouchTone registration system but also offer students an automatic schedule builder feature. Students would no longer be required to search through the class schedule for open or available sections. Course preferences would only need to be entered and, based on the student time preferences or time blocks, the system would then proceed to build a variety of potential schedules. The desired features of a schedule builder needed to include:

- Saved working drafts
- Any registered courses
- Available 24/7
- Schedule by course, not by section
- Display output in calendar format and honor time blocks

The project team included the following groups:

- Programmers from the Student Information System
- Web developers
- Dean of Academic Records and Registrar and key staff from the Registrar's Office
- Selected students from the Student Senate

All the design and development was completed "in house," so there was no cost associated with the project.

Students and advisors benefited immeasurably from the implementation of the new system. In the past, academic advisors were required to spend valuable time with students searching throughout the class schedule for open sections. Advisors now have the opportunity to spend more time with students planning their academic programs. Students once needed to constantly check computer output reports for available course sections, or attempt to add open classes one section at a time using the TouchTone system. When the system was first released to the student body of 30,000 in the spring 2002 semester, approximately 19,000 students used the new Web-based system to either process their original registrations or add classes to their programs.

Figure 10.2 demonstrates a student's completed schedule.

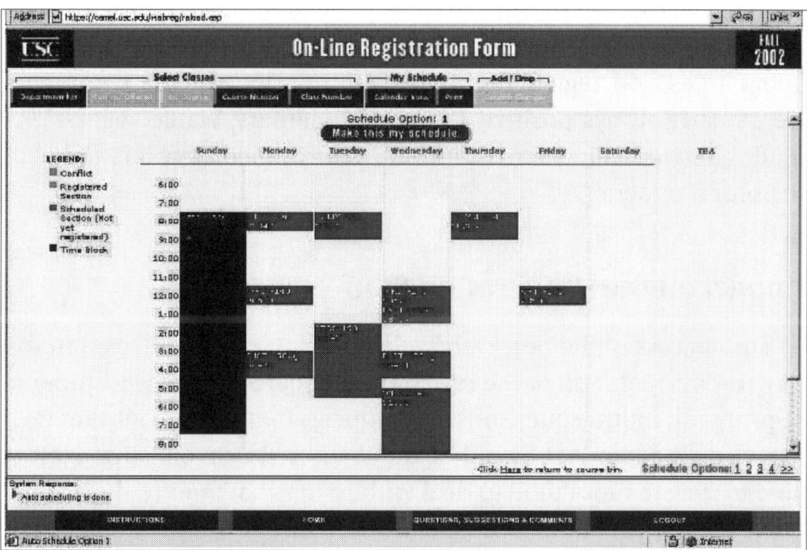

Figure 10.2 Student Schedule

Upon the system's initial release, we sent e-mail messages to students who used the new Web system, thanked them for their participation, and asked them to verify the results of their transactions. Based on a variety of responses and inquiries, it was soon realized that students needed a detailed summary or receipt of their interaction with the Web. Within three months, we changed the program to send each student user a total summary or description of all transactions each time Web registration was used. The service significantly reduced the number of phone calls and e-mail inquiries. I would recommend that this type of message or communication be implemented the moment the system is released.

The success of the project was reflected in three basic areas: student usage and satisfaction; impact on the registration staff; and general reaction from the academic advisement community.

Student Usage

When the new Web registration system was announced to the entire student body, the response was 99 percent favorable. Reports of usage problems were minimal and comments were always positive. An e-mail account was initially attached to the Web process and students were given the option to respond with comments and questions each time the system was used. Besides the routine questions about rules and regulations related to enrollment, the comments were nearly always positive and complimentary. Viable suggestions made about enhancements continue to be immediately forwarded to the programmers.

Impact on the Registration Staff

The success of the new Web registration system is reflected in the day-to-day operation of the registration department. Fewer students appear with routine questions and requests for transactions that now can easily be handled by either the Web or TouchTone. The staff is able to devote more time to deal with issues that require their assistance or interpretation, and spend more time with the 5 percent of the student body who are prohibited from using the automated enrollment systems.

Advisement Community

Advisers enthusiastically reported the impact on their offices. The auto scheduler feature of the new Web system has freed advisors from needing to spend arduous hours with students searching for available class sections. The new system has given them the opportunity to spend more quality time with students and increased their ability to concentrate on purely academic issues. Advisors have also reported on the success and accuracy factor of student usage. The academic community claims that the new system is far more user-friendly than TouchTone and offers fewer chances of making data entry errors.

Careful planning and thorough testing are two important elements involved in ensuring the success of such a project. Advice to other schools considering such a project includes:

1. Obtain administrative approval: If necessary to obtain administrative approval for the funding and programming support of such a project, submit a written proposal to senior administration. The proposal should contain a list of the desired features and a conceptual overview of the proposed system.

2. Appoint planning and focus groups: A successful planning group must contain a cross section of your best students, programmers, Web developers, and administrators. Throughout the development of the project, the group needs to establish a timeline of goals and must meet on a regular basis. Focus groups, including faculty and students, help validate that the final product met the intentions and expectations of the community.

3. Consider all desired features: In designing the system consider all the desired features needed to offer students maximum service and convenience. These features should include an efficient and comprehensive schedule builder component; links to the curriculum information; links to the schedule of classes; access to degree audit analysis; link to student course guide; and display of final examination schedules. Instructions should be written

clearly and the processes should be as user-friendly as possible.

4. Before releasing the system for student usage, test the new processes thoroughly. Invite your best and most seasoned advisors and Registrar's staff to participate, and include student groups to test and make any needed suggestions. When using advisors and Registrar's staff as a test population, provide them with a variety of test records and ask them to test all registration edits and every enrollment combination possible. Analyze the testing results and recommendations carefully since potential problems and system "bugs" are often discovered and easily remedied in this manner.

5. Communication strategies for announcing new system: Offer scheduled information sessions for the university community that include a thorough demonstration of the new system. Ensure that all academic advisors are invited, as they will tend to be your biggest supporters and allies in launching and implementing a new system. Mail or e-mail all currently enrolled students and announce the release of the new system. Include an e-mail address with the Web process. Establish a ruling that any inquiries received through the Web e-mail process are answered within 24 hours. It is also highly recommended that students be notified via e-mail each time the Web registration process is used to enroll or change a program. The message should contain a summary of the transactions entered.

Testing the system thoroughly was a guarantee toward releasing a product that proved to be nearly 100 percent accurate and dependable. Communication strategies were extremely effective in engaging the support of the entire university community. Sixteen open forum sessions were presented on both campuses and all academic advisors and student affairs officers were invited to attend. Immediate notification of each Web transaction via e-mail to students proved to be an excellent communication tool.

CHAPTER 11

E-Relationships: Enriching Communication with Prospective Students

Suzanne Petrusch
Director of Marketing for Enrollment Management
University of Dayton

The University of Dayton was founded in 1850 by the Society of Mary, commonly referred to as the Marianists, a teaching order of Catholic priests and brothers. The university, with 6,500 full-time undergraduate students and a total enrollment of 10,100, is the largest private university in the state of Ohio. The College of Arts and Sciences and the schools of business administration, education and allied professions, engineering, and law constitute the academic structure.

Named one of the most significant campus sites in the country by the American Society of Landscape Architects, the University of Dayton's 123-acre campus provides an array of resources designed to enable the academic, personal, and spiritual growth of the students. The university was selected by the Templeton Foundation as one of 100 colleges and universities that encourages character development and prepares students for lives of personal and civic responsibility.

Two distinct honors programs, with more than $15 million in independent endowment, are offered to the most academically accomplished students. The University Honors and John W. Berry, Sr. Scholars Program are designed to enhance every undergraduate degree program. The programs offer a means for students to seek an enriched academic experience that encourages development of their intellectual and creative gifts.

Professors are committed to teaching undergraduate students. The undergraduate population is a traditional student body with the majority of students entering directly from high school. According to results of the Admitted Student Questionnaire (ASQ) and other survey instruments, students choose the university because it is academically challenging, comfortable, friendly, and fun. With the vast majority of students living in university housing, it is easy for them to be engaged in service learning, campus ministry, professional and social organizations in addition to their academic pursuits. Students prepare for their careers through a variety of opportunities including internships, cooperative education, and cultural immersion experiences. An active campus social environment balances the rigor of the classroom.

Under the leadership of Chris Muñoz, former vice president for enrollment management, the enrollment management division at the University of Dayton decided to seize the opportunity to gain a competitive advantage based on strategic use of the World Wide Web. In the mid-1990s the Internet was exploding as a means of delivering information and services. The premise was to use the Web as a tool for relationship development with an audience that we predicted to be most receptive—teenagers who grew up in the information and video game age.

Three primary objectives shaped the decision to invest in a Web strategy for recruitment at the undergraduate level. The first was to gain a competitive advantage in the marketplace. The second was to achieve enrollment and net revenue goals. The third was to shape the academic profile of the entering first-year class.

Prior to 1996 the Office of Admission, one unit within the enrollment management division, operated a basic informational Web site. The transformation to a transactional model began when a partnership was formed with three University of Dayton students who founded a Web design company then known as Cyber Design (now LiquidMatrix) founded in 1996. The students, Kyle Burkholder, Kevin Guyton, and David Marshall, proposed an interactive site that would appeal to the University of Dayton's traditional teenage market. The leadership in enrollment management quickly embraced the idea and began to collaborate with the Cyber Design team. Guyton and Marshall lead a firm of 28 employees based in Buffalo, New York. The core product is ActiveCampus, an integrated suite of

Web-based software applications that enables institutions to communicate with external constituents via the Web.

As the admission site evolved, a parallel development was occurring within the academic leadership in 1997. A concept termed the Learning Village was being developed as a metaphor for delivering various types of connected learning. The impetus behind the Learning Village was to allow students to see linkages to the greater world beyond the campus environment. A critical component of the Learning Village is the infrastructure that was built to support a technology-enhanced learning environment. In addition to fully wiring the campus including the residence halls for high-speed Internet access, the university tackled the ambitious project of wiring the student neighborhood, the equivalent of wiring 25 city blocks. To support the goal of developing distinctive graduates, the university calculated the need for all students regardless of major to have a skill set that would include the use of personal computers, productivity software, collaborative tools, and online research capabilities. This bold experiment required a paradigm shift among the faculty, and a willingness to redesign curriculum so that faculty and students could engage in new means of exploring knowledge. In order for all students to have equal access to technology, the decision was made to require a computer purchase by all full-time entering students. Under the leadership of Thomas Skill, Ph.D., associate provost for educational technology and associate CIO and codirector of the Learning Village, several models of deployment were explored, and the decision was made to have all students purchase a personal computer from among a set of designated units. Tangent Computer, Inc. of Burlingame, California, has served as the university's partner in the initiative since its inception. The challenge for the counselors in the Office of Admission was to explain the value proposition behind the technology-enhanced learning and student computer initiative to prospective students, their families, and other constituents.

The strategic objective that emerged for enrollment management was to determine how the admission Web site could be used as part of a twofold plan. The first part of the plan was to gain operational efficiencies in the Office of Admission through a combination of use of the Internet and the implementation of document imaging. The second part of the plan entailed giving prospective students the chance to experience a glimpse of the technology-enhanced learning environment by creating appropriate experiences through the admission and related Web sites. The tactical components evolved through the vision of the enrollment management Web team, led Muñoz and Suzanne Petrusch, director of marketing for enrollment management, and LiquidMatrix.

Permission marketing, a term coined by Seth Godin, is an approach to marketing based on building ongoing relationships by sharing information the customer has requested. Permission marketing is sometimes referred to as opt-in marketing. Using the concept of permission marketing, the primary component of the admission Web site is personalization. Prospective students are invited to personalize the site and join the electronic mail list. When the site is personalized, it welcomes the user by name and displays feature stories and current student profiles tagged to academic and extracurricular interests indicated by the user. A to-do list guides the student through tasks specific to various stages of the enrollment funnel. Figures 11.1–11.4 illustrate how personalization works on the University of Dayton admission site.

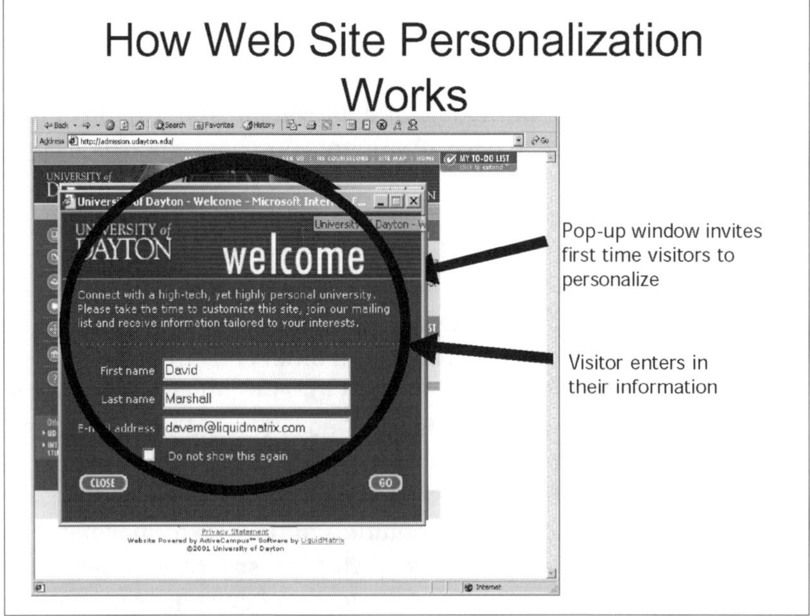

Figure 11.1 Web Site Personalization

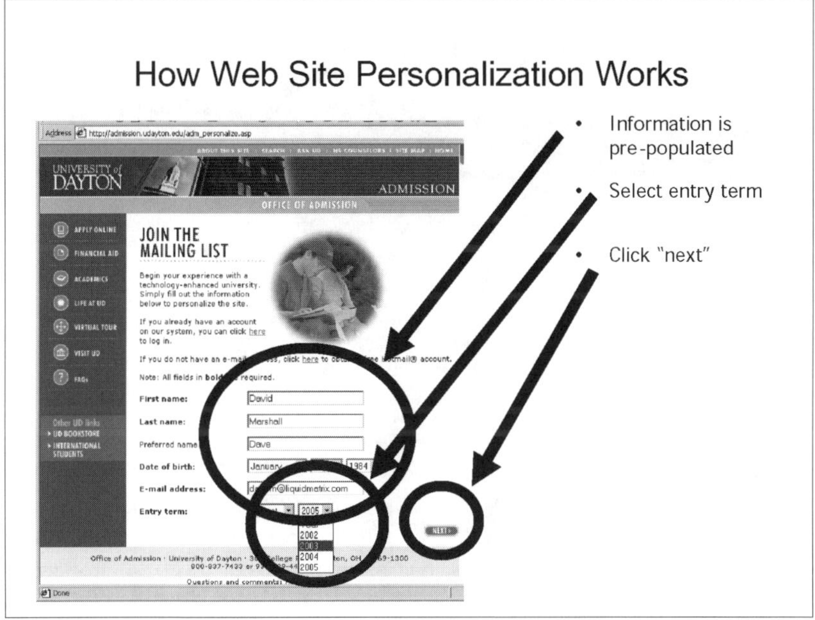

Figure 11.2 Information Is Prepopulated from the Database

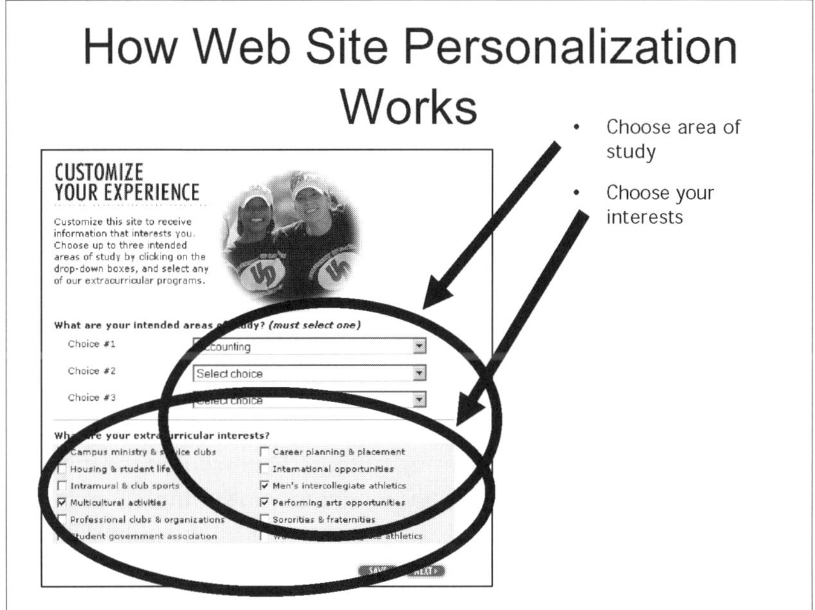

Figure 11.3 Areas of Interest Are Specified

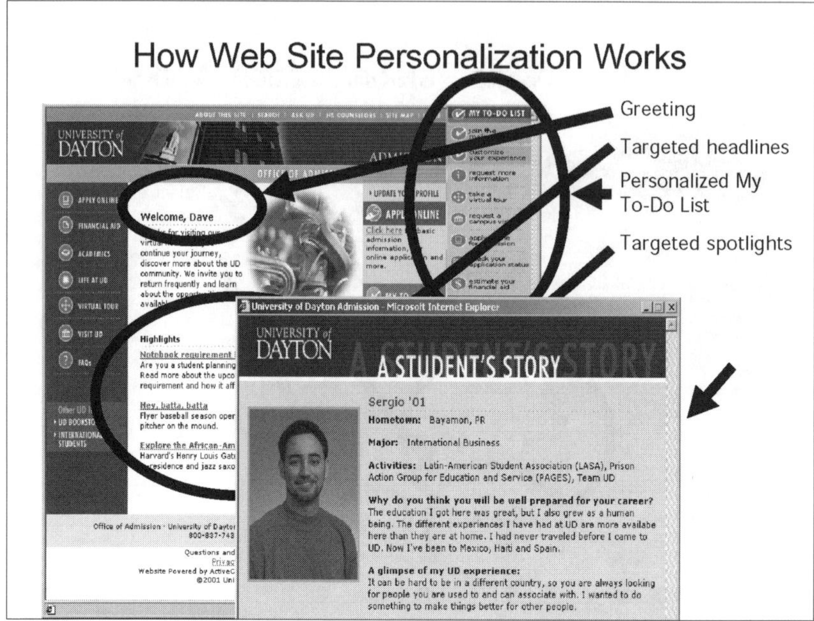

Figure 11.4 The Personalized Web Page Appears

Other features of the admission Web site include an online application for admission and scholarship, an application status check, a financial need estimator, and a campus visit request form. The first online version of the application launched in January of 1997. The majority of applications for the following fall term are realized before January, and the online application was not advertised in the first year due to the timing of the launch in comparison to the applicant pool generation. However, 2 percent of the students who applied for the term beginning in August 1997 did so online. They had the initiative to find the application without any direction from the University of Dayton. The following year, a concerted effort was made to publicize the online application, and an incentive of no application fee was made known. For the class entering in 1998, 28 percent of the applications were submitted electronically. Students who submitted an online application had a slightly better academic profile as measured by test scores compared with the students who completed paper applications. By 2001 more than 60 percent of the first-year applications to the University were being filed online. In a bold experiment, the university declared the only way for a first-year student to apply would be online through the university's secure application.

People who did not see the potential value of the Web as a tool to communicate with teenagers through a medium for which they expressed preference, questioned if the growing applicant pool was soft. They speculated that the lack of a fee caused students who would otherwise never have applied to frivolously file an application with the University of Dayton. Several metrics were monitored carefully to ensure the validity of the results. Muñoz and Petrusch found that students who applied online yielded at a higher rate than students who applied by the traditional paper method. In enrollment management terminology, "conversion" is used to describe movement from the inquiry to applicant stage in the enrollment funnel while "yield" refers to enrollment at the institution.

Additional speculation was raised as to whether or not the University of Dayton was discriminating against students of color and students from lower socioeconomic levels. When a choice between two methods of application existed, African-American students applied online at a higher rate than Caucasian students. The enrollment management team studied application rates by methods across various socioeconomic levels, and using data from the Free Application for Federal Students Aid (FAFSA), found that there was no difference in online application rates between high-income and low-income students. Muñoz and Petrusch looked beyond the results for their own institution to watch the larger trends. According to studies conducted by the art and science group, the Web was becoming the pervasive method for students to seek information regarding colleges and universities. Perhaps more importantly, the studies showed the lack of a digital divide among the college-bound population. The national trends confirmed what was being experienced by the University of Dayton as an advantage in meeting the enrollment goals of the institution.

While the admission Web strategy cannot be isolated as the only determinant factor for the success the University of Dayton experienced from 1996 to present, it is believed to have played an extremely important role. From 1996 to 2003 (as of July 22, 2003), the applicant pool increased by 53.4 percent. During that same period, the number of deposits increased by 20.9 percent. With much weight being given to the importance of financial strength, the university realized a net revenue gain of 70.1 percent.

Measuring specific components of the online strategy, the team had evidence that personalization of the site and use of the financial need estimator resulted in application rates well in excess of the standard inquiry to application conversion rate. The URL of the admission site is boldly presented in all print materials, and messages are crafted to demonstrate the value of technology, both in the admission process and as part of the University of Dayton student experience. In addition to a marriage between print and electronic communication, the team experimented with three strategies to drive traffic to the Web.

The first strategy focused on cultivation of a strong prospect pool well matched to the university. Prospects are defined within enrollment management as students in whom the institution has interest regardless of whether the student is familiar with the institution. Collaborating with LipmanHearne and abeedle.com, Petrusch led a strategy to direct prospects to highly personalized Web sites commonly referred to as microsites. LipmanHearne, a strategic positioning and communications firm specializing in work with nonprofit institutions, approached the enrollment leadership team at UD with a pitch for a new communication strategy directed at high school juniors. With a growing reputation for being a leader in the use of technology as a recruitment tool, the University of Dayton has been a desired partner for organizations desiring to launch new e-marketing products and services. LipmanHearne arranged for abeedle.com, a recruitment marketing and e-communication firm, to create the microsites and broadcast the e-mail messages. A URL tied to the University of Dayton domain identifies each site and contains the prospective student's first and last names. When the student visits the microsite, data regarding the student's preferences and navigation is captured. Through various microsite features, the student is driven to the UD admission site. The back end tool provided by abeedle.com tracks visit rates to the microsites, and the data is presented in an online report for the client.

In 2002, the first year during which UD used this prospect Web strategy, the prospect pool was divided in thirds according to model scores calculated through use of Noel-Levitz' predictive modeling tool, Forecast*Plus*. The higher the model score, the greater is the student's propensity to enroll at the University of Dayton. Messages were segmented by in-state or out-of-state location, attendance at a Catholic or other type of high school, and general area of academic interest. Students in the highest model score range received large format post cards. Each card was printed on an Indigo press with the student's name and personal URL. Those in the middle score range received a high impact letter containing the URL in three locations within the body as well as on the envelope. Students whose model scores fell within the lowest third received only an HTML e-mail message with a link to the microsite. No communication was sent to a student in the bottom model score segment if the university did receive an e-mail address in the prospect record. Figure 11.5 shows the large format postcard sent to students with high model scores. Figure 11.6 depicts the high impact letter sent to students in the middle range of model scores, while Figure 11.7 illustrates the HTML e-mail message initially sent only to students in the bottom score segment.

Anticipating the behavior predicted by the model, the team expected the highest response rates to come from the top model score group. The low model score group visited the microsites at a rate of 11.6 percent. The top model score group exhibited a visit rate of 7.2 percent while the middle group lagged at a mere 5.7 percent. Confident in the mathematical validity of the model, the team reassessed the methods of contact. They delivered the personalized HTML e-mail message to every student in the top and middle score groups for whom an e-mail address was on file. Response rates changed in alignment with the model when the traditional direct mail message was reinforced with electronic communication. Prospects in the high model score group achieved a response rate of 15.1 percent and the middle model score group improved by seven percent to reach a 12.7 percent response rate.

The second strategy to drive traffic to the Web was proposed by Rich Wicklund of Avideon, a technology-based direct response marketing firm located in Baltimore. Having a base of corporate clients, Wicklund pitched his idea to Muñoz with the hope of a University of Dayton partnership opening the door to the university market. Wicklund's team worked with Petrusch to develop an interactive CD designed to lead prospective students to the Web. The CD incorporated a Flash introduction created by LiquidMatrix. Working with Glenn Walters, media executive-in-residence in UD's department of communication, Petrusch provided Avideon with robust content including video and voice. Jeff Ohl of P.S. Creative designed a CD

How Do We Contact Them?
Personalized Postcard

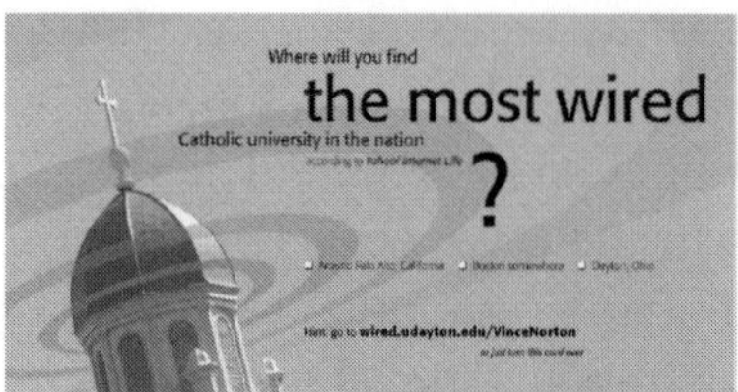

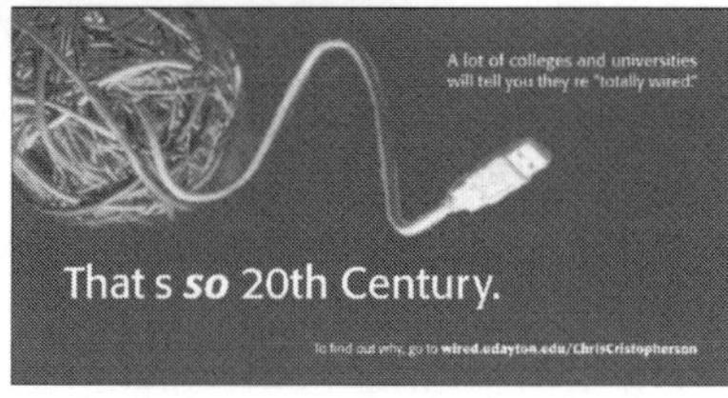

Figure 11.5 Using Personalized Information to Contact Students

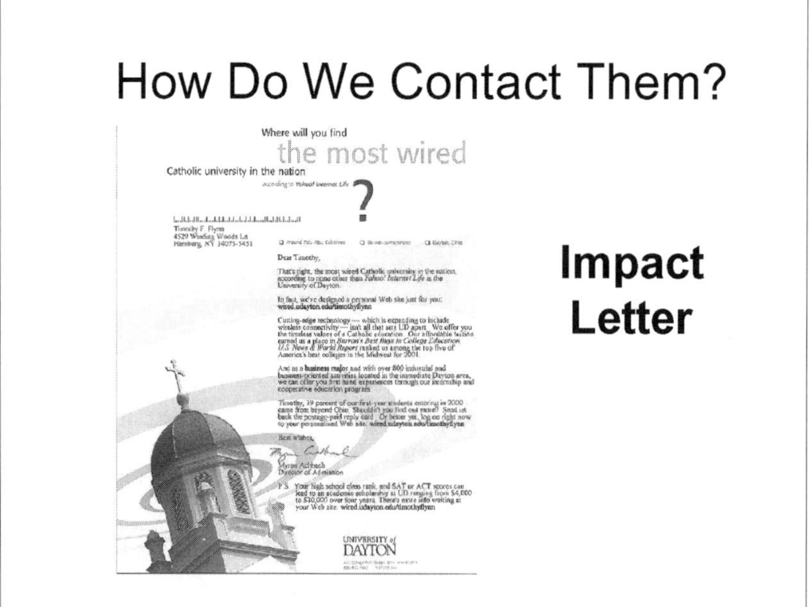

Where will you find
the most wired
Catholic university in the nation
according to Yahoo! Internet Life
?

Timothy F. Flynn
4529 Winding Woods La
Hamburg, NY 14075-5451

Dear Timothy,

That's right, the most wired Catholic university in the nation, according to none other than *Yahoo! Internet Life* is the University of Dayton.

In fact, we've designed a personal Web site just for you: **wired.udayton.edu/timothyflynn**

Cutting-edge technology — which is expanding to include wireless connectivity — isn't all that sets UD apart. We offer you the timeless values of a Catholic education. Our affordable tuition earned us a place in *Barron's Best Buys in College Education*. *U.S. News & World Report* ranked us among the top five of America's best colleges in the Midwest for 2001.

And as a **business major** and with over 800 industrial and business-oriented activities located in the immediate Dayton area, we can offer you first hand experiences through our internship and cooperative education program.

Timothy, 39 percent of our first-year students entering in 2000 came from beyond Ohio. Shouldn't you find out more? Send us back the postage-paid reply card. Or better yet, log on right now to your personalized Web site: **wired.udayton.edu/timothyflynn**

Best wishes,

Myron Achbach
Director of Admission

P.S. Your high school class rank, and SAT or ACT scores can lead to an academic scholarship at UD ranging from $4,000 to $30,000 over four years. There's more info waiting at your Web site: wired.udayton.edu/timothyflynn

UNIVERSITY of DAYTON

Figure 11.6 The Impact Letter

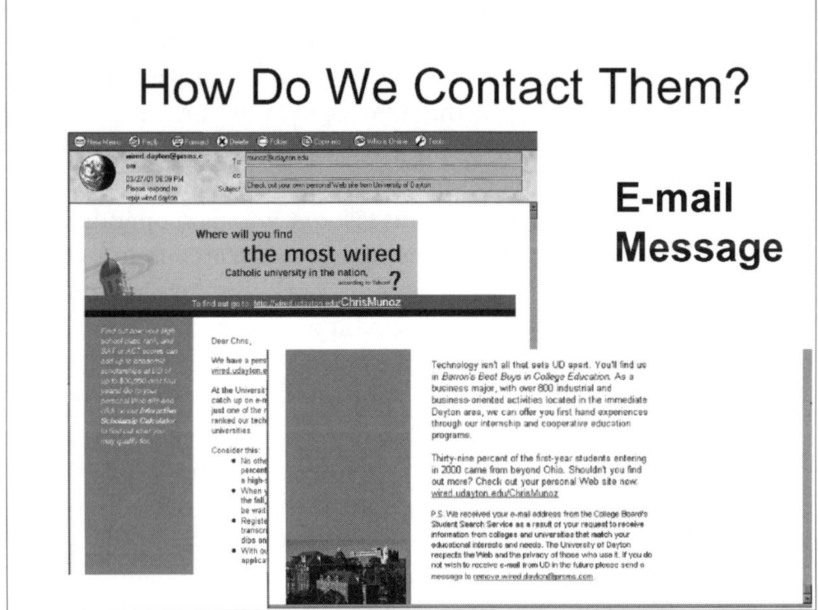

Figure 11.7 E-Mail Contact

mailer that reflected the images and messages contained in the Flash introduction.

Avideon's statistical reporting tool allowed the University of Dayton team to monitor the effectiveness of this promotional effort by downloading user data, counting the click rate per hot link, and measuring repeat visits. Further, follow-up electronic communication plans based on student interests as interpreted through use of the CD and admission Web site, were executed through the Avideon tool. While those students who used the CD took full advantage of the features, Muñoz and Petrusch determined that the overall response rate to the CD did not warrant further investment.

However, one component of the CD did serve as the inspiration for the third method of driving prospective student traffic to the Web. The University of Dayton team decided to incorporate the Flash introduction from the CD into an e-mail message that would be sent to elicit a certain response from students within the inquiry pool. Inquiries are students who have indicated an interest in the institution. LiquidMatrix was retained to alter the Flash file. They shortened the video and sound sequence, and added a splash page to the end of the Flash experience. The splash page can be modified by the University of Dayton's creative staff to vary the text and include links to any area of the admission Web site. Through the ActiveAdmission console, enrollment management staff track the results of each Flash e-mail sent. Statistics include counts of total visitors, distinct visitors, anonymous visitors, and data on individual users. The click rate for the initial campaign was relatively low at 6.45 percent. However, of the users who did click, the application rate was 26.5 percent. Every communication is designed to inspire the recipient to move through the stages of the enrollment funnel. In determining when and how to continue to use the Flash e-mail message, the team focused on the 26.5 percent conversion rate that exceeded the norm from inquiry to applicant. The university continues to use the Flash e-mail making sure a student receives the message only once during the inquiry stage.

Prospective students remain the primary target audience of the University of Dayton's Web strategy; however, in an effort to embrace the high school guidance community, UD teamed with LiquidMatrix to develop a guidance counselor resource center within the admission site. The motivation was the anticipation of resistance by a segment of the guidance community to the online application requirement. The premise was to reduce resistance by sharing a glimpse of the university's high-tech, high touch environment. Information regarding the status of applicants from a given school is available to the counselor around the clock. To use the site, counselors must request access by submitting first and last names, high school CEEB code, and telephone number via a form on the Web. Although e-mail is not a required field, the information is requested. An e-mail notification informs Petrusch's staff that a counselor has requested access. To take every measure to alleviate security concerns, a telephone call is then placed to the counselor at the place of employment to verify his or her identity. Using the ActiveAdmission console, Petrusch's staff creates a user name and generates a random password to provide to the counselor. The counselor is then ready to log in to the secure area of the admission site to gather information on the applicants to the University of Dayton from that high school. Counselors do not have access to information regarding any student attending another school.

A high school counselor using the site sees summary information on the first screen and a list of all applicants with the application status of each. By clicking on any name within the list, the counselor moves to a detail page indicating the major to which the student applied, the application date, a list of any missing items, the decision if complete, and comments. With the public's ever increasing interest in privacy issues, Petrusch was careful to review the plans for the tool with Leroy Rooker of the FERPA office. Per Rooker, the University of Dayton was within the guidelines for appropriate disclosure of information to individual guidance counselors. Usage patterns have closely mimicked the composition of the University of Dayton's first-year class. Approximately 60 percent of the counselors using the tool are from Ohio, with the next largest group representing Illinois.

The efforts of enrollment management to engage students in a relationship with the university through the Web are just the beginning of what a student preparing to enter the University of Dayton will experience. After students indicate their intent to attend the university by completing the online enrollment confirmation process, including submission of a $300 enrollment deposit, they are invited to participate in Virtual Orientation (VO). The VO concept stemmed from the desire to use technology to support and enhance community building and connected learning, facilitate and enrich the transition from high school to college life, and provide a highly personalized, dynamic online educational and social orientation.

Mr. Marcus Robinson, director of development and strategy for the College of Arts and Sciences and Educational Information Technology Internet Development Division and Web Partnership, built a talented team that could deliver an interactive experience to the deposited students. For the students who entered UD in 2001, the inaugural year of VO provided announcements, answers to frequently asked questions, a parents' section, academic resources, language placement exams, personal profile with messaging and chat capabilities, a bookstore interface, customizable personal space, and an introduction to the humanities base curriculum. In that first year, the 20-week lifespan of the site saw approximately 1,750 users who averaged 22 minutes per login. In total, there were approximately 4,000 logins per week, and the top 10 users averaged 17 logins per week. Seventeen thousand messages were exchanged between incoming students and 9,600 chat sessions were launched. Through an evolution, VO has erupted into a full-blown interactive experience designed to prepare students for meaningful integration into the University of Dayton learning community.

In 2002 Robinson and his team redesigned the user interface, expanded the placement exams, included a word-and-phrase search utility, enhanced the academic orientation and social interaction components, created a schedule wizard for the New Student Orientation Program, and more. Virtual orientation was never intended to replace the on-campus New Student Orientation Program. Rather, VO serves a complementary role in the overall strategy of building a student community and a relationship with the university that will extend beyond the time of graduation.

CHAPTER 12

Institutional Strategy and Information Support: The Role of Data Warehousing in Higher Education

Jeff Guan, Associate Professor,
Department of Computer Information Systems
William Nunez, Associate Director,
Office of Planning and Budget and
John F. Welsh, Associate Provost and Associate Professor,
Department of Leadership and Foundations,
University of Louisville

The University of Louisville is a state supported, metropolitan research and teaching institution with three campuses located in Louisville, Kentucky. The university enrolls approximately 21,000 students and offers a comprehensive array of degrees at the bachelor's, master's, and doctoral level. The university has a health sciences campus comprised of schools of medicine, dentistry, nursing, and public health. Colleges and schools in arts and sciences, engineering, law, music, social work, and education are located at the University's Belknap campus. Continuing and community education programs are offered at the Shelby Campus.

A Context for Change

Colleges and universities today face three common challenges that are prompting a critical reexamination of the architecture, management, and use of their information systems: First, administrators and policy makers at all levels demand improved data management strategies to support resource management and strategic planning. Second, due to a changed competitive environment for higher education as a whole, faculty and administrators are hungry for information that can assist institutions in the recruitment and retention of students. Third, external oversight agencies, such as the federal government, state governments, and accrediting agencies demand information about the performance of institutions and programs on a wide array of indicators. At issue is the extent to which existing information systems and knowledge management strategies optimize the ability of institutions to respond to a new environment.

Advances in technology have dramatically enhanced the level of productivity and efficiency of universities and colleges, forever altering the way universities operate. However, despite the availability of powerful computers, advanced network and communication infrastructures, and sophisticated software applications, university decision makers, including planning and budget administrators, still lack access to the critical information necessary for informed decision making. Deans and provosts often lament lack of access to valid and reliable information about their finances, staffing, and students. Ironically, the information they require frequently exists in the organization. However, only a fraction of the data that are captured, processed, and stored in a college or university's information system are actually available to decision makers in an organized manner.

This chapter examines the root causes of information problems from the perspective of decision makers. It assesses data warehousing as a solution to decision support and knowledge management in higher education. The chapter first looks at the need for data-driven decision making in higher education and then explains why typical information technology architectures found in higher education fail to meet the needs for decision making. The chapter next discusses how data warehousing functions as knowledge management through the organization of mountains of data residing in campus information systems.

Institutional Issues

Ideally, organizational decision making begins with an in-depth analysis of available management information. Decision makers then use information to weigh alternatives, analyze options, anticipate implications, and project outcomes within the context of their organization and environment. If, however, decision makers lack relevant, reliable, and timely information, the quality and credibility of their decisions is suspect.

Higher education has always been a dynamic environment requiring strong leadership and solid decision making, but the current pace of change in higher education forces leaders to seek rapid access to information to expedite decision making. Leaders in education are frequently required to consider many variables simultaneously as well as their impact of decisions on internal and external constituencies. These variables and constituencies fall into four broad categories to consider: a) complexities of the organization; b) vast number of stakeholders and appraisers; c) competitive marketplace; and d) resource limitations.

Complexities of the Organization

Higher education institutions vary widely in their organizational structure and administrative and governance systems. Generally, however, colleges and universities share governance with a plethora of constituents. Birnbaum (1988) classifies these structures as either "loosely coupled," "tightly coupled," or some variant between. Birnbaum suggests that governance and management procedures should exist that address the specific "economic, social value, political, informational, and physical characteristics" of the institution and its environment (p. 43). The decision-making subsystems within institutions require vast amounts of quality information to address the requirements of the environment. Frequently, demands for information about the programs and services of an institution go unanswered because information management systems cannot respond.

Stakeholders

Depending on the type and size of the institution, stakeholders evaluate the quality of the institution, rate the programs, or impact institutional policy. These stakeholders include agencies from state coordinating boards, to accrediting bodies, to institutional rankings by *U.S. News and World Report*. These agencies all require detailed information regarding admissions, student demographics, program effectiveness, student outcomes, and many other measures. Additionally, decision makers must consider the impact of decisions on internal stakeholders at their institutions. While the number of the stakeholders is inevitably linked to the size and type of institution, they generally include students, parents, faculty, staff, board members, legislators, and community leaders. Information systems must provide institutional decision makers with access to quality data for and about each of these constituent groups.

Competitive Marketplace

College students have many choices available to them today. The new competition in the educational marketplace has forced institutions to be more focused and competitive as they attempt to recruit these potential students. In an effort to capture the "best and brightest" of these students, proactive institutions have implemented sophisticated marketing campaigns and focused recruitment plans to define their niche in the educational marketplace. Building a successful marketing plan or recruitment campaign requires detailed understanding of the pool of qualified applicants. Questions about the potential pool of students are answered by data available in most institutional databases that, once transformed into management information, becomes a powerful resource decision makers can use to combat market pressures and increased competition. If this information is not readily available to decision makers, the institution will struggle in defining its customer base, service area, core competencies, and other aspects necessary for an integrated marketing plan.

Resource Limitations

As operating costs increase, strain on the budget follows as institutional leaders struggle to balance the academic and human resources needs of colleges and universities. As state support stays at levels of inflation and increased emphasis is placed on student tuition and fees and external funding, decision makers are forced to determine which programs are critical, in high demand, and/or operating at a lower cost per student. Institutions are also concerned about program efficiencies and resource management. An analysis of how to optimize resource management can only be achieved through an integration of data from both financial and student systems to evaluate the costs of operating vs. the benefit received from those investments. The characteristics of information needs of today's institutional decision makers can be summarized as:

- The information required often has to be derived from a vast amount of data.
- The information required is often integrated from diverse internal and external data sources.
- Historical data are often necessary to understand trends.
- Rapid response is necessary for decision makers.
- Information requests are often ad hoc in nature.

The Structure and Scope of Data Warehouses in Higher Education

The existing information technology (IT) infrastructures at many organizations are inadequate to meet the information needs of institutional decision makers. There are two main causes for this lack of adequate decision support. The first has to do with the nature of many of the existing IT systems. The second cause lies in the often poorly integrated IT architecture.

Colleges and universities have invested heavily in IT over the past few decades, including more recent investments in Web-based technologies. Most of these IT systems have one thing in common: they have been acquired to support the day-to-day operations. Such systems are often referred to as online transaction processing (OLTP) systems. An OLTP environment is not suitable for decision support as these systems have been designed to support short transactions affecting a few records at a time. This type of data tends to reflect only the current state of the system and seldom keeps historical snapshots, which are critical for planning purposes.

Due to the types of transactions an OLTP system supports, different kinds of data tend to be scattered in different tables. For example, with PeopleSoft software a simple class list report with class data, meeting times, building, instructor, and student data may require the integration of data from more than 30 different tables (PeopleSoft, 2001). Extracting and integrating information from all these tables are not only time-consuming, the process requires very complicated programming. Additionally, the pertinent data reside in different systems or databases. Finally, the day-to-day operations performed by an OLTP system often are already constraining the hardware and software resources on the system. Adding a decision support function on top of an OLTP system can severely impact its performance. Decision support queries involve thousands and often millions of records and are extremely resource intensive.

A less obvious reason why many IT infrastructures are inadequate for decision support has to do with the naturally evolved information technology (IT) architecture found in many organizations today (Inmon, 1996; Linthicum, 2000). IT investments often come in the form of one application at a time, with little integration or interoperability in mind. New applications and new technologies are often introduced into the existing IT architecture in a hurry to meet an urgent business need or in an effort to catch up with competitors. This kind of natural evolution of an IT architecture eventually results in a set of extremely complex and incompatible systems, leading to enterprisewide data and information chaos (see Figure 12.1).

From a decision support perspective, this kind of poorly integrated architecture leads to several problems that affect any data-driven decision making. The most common problems are data extraction

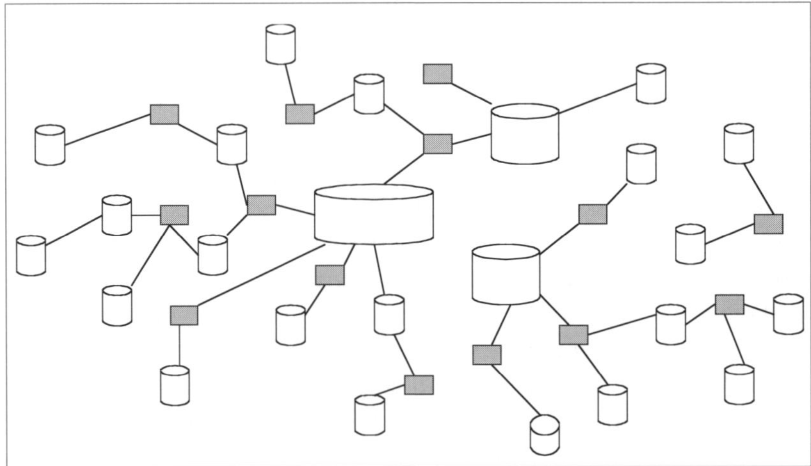

Figure 12.1 Information Chaos

costs and lack of data consistency. Customized extraction programs frequently have to be written to extract, cleanse, reconcile, and integrate the data. There is often more than one path to obtaining the same type of report. Hence, different offices produce different results to the same inquiry.

Data Warehousing

A separate environment is needed for decision support. Although decision support systems have been around for many years, it was not until the early 1990s that they were labeled "data warehouses." The most commonly used definition of data warehouse is "an integrated, subject-oriented, time-variant, nonvolatile database that provides support for decision making" (Inmon, 1996). The meaning of each of these terms for decision support is pertinent to this discussion.

- *Integrated.* The data warehouse is a centralized, consolidated database that integrates data derived from the entire organization. Thus the data warehouse consolidates data from multiple and diverse formats. Data integration implies a well-organized effort to define and standardize all data elements. This integration effort can be time-consuming but, once accomplished, it provides a unified view of the overall organization.

- *Subject-oriented.* Data warehouse data are arranged and optimized to provide answers to questions coming from diverse functional areas within an organization. Therefore, the data warehouse contains data organized and summarized by topic, such as student demographics and human resources. This type of data organization is very different from that found in a typical OLTP system.

- *Time-variant.* In contrast to OLTP systems that focus on current transactions, the data warehouse data represents historical data as well as current transactions. It is also time-variant in the sense that once the data are periodically loaded to the data warehouse all time-dependent aggregations are recomputed.

- *Nonvolatile.* Once data enters the data warehouse, they are never removed. The reasoning: the data in the data

> warehouse represent the organization's entire history, the operational data, representing the near-term history, are always added to it. Because data are never deleted and new data are always added, the data warehouse is always expanding.

A data warehouse provides a solution to meeting the information needs of institutional decision makers. The data source component represents all of the sources from which the raw data originate. To identify the data sources, candidate systems and files are scrutinized and evaluated in terms of integrity and quality of data. The data acquisition component captures data from the source systems and directs them into the data warehouse. This is often the most complicated and critical component of data warehousing. Rules must be defined that guide the cleansing, enhancement, restructuring, integration, and aggregation of source data. Data cleansing may involve the restructuring of records or fields, removal of operational-only data, supply of missing field values, and checking of data integrity and consistency.

Data enhancement may involve decoding and translating field values, adding a time-attribute to reflect the currency of data, summarizing data, or calculating derived values. The definitions created for the data during the data acquisition process will be stored as metadata, which will be used later in the data warehouse system for generating reports and analytics.

The data warehouse component is often one or several databases that contain the data warehouse information. The data warehouse contains a large data repository called the enterprise data warehouse and several smaller data warehouses, called data marts, as indicated in Figure 12.2. The enterprise data warehouse usually contains enterprisewide data that provides an enterprise view of the organization. An enterprise view of data provides an integrated view of the data of an organization. This enterprise representation of data is created by gathering data from the various departments/lines of business. The data have been standardized, cleansed, and integrated. Such an enterprise view of data provides a view of the entire organization that would be difficult or impossible to obtain by looking at the data each individual department has. The data marts are often data repositories that focus on data collections and analysis of interest to specific user communities, such as budget and planning, human resource, and

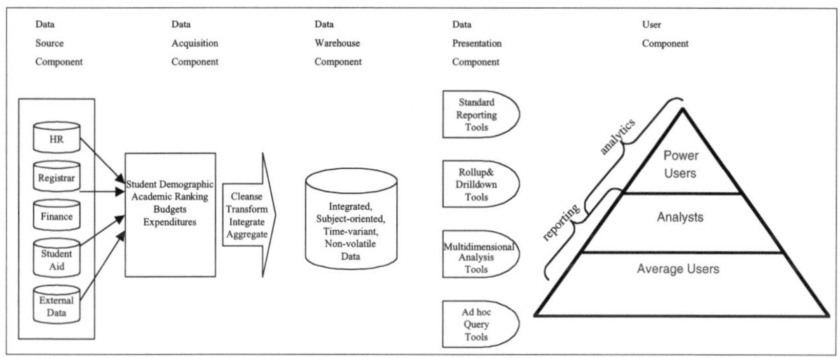

Figure 12.2 Architecture of a Typical Data Warehouse System

students. In addition to holding cleansed, integrated, historical, and aggregated data, the data warehouse also structures data in ways that make analysis easier.

The presentation component is the most visible component, as users interact with the data warehouse system through it. This component is often implemented with tools referred to as business intelligence (BI) tools. The presentation component represents different levels of services from simple reporting to roll-up and drill-down functionality to multidimensional analysis to true ad hoc query capability. What is worth mentioning in particular is the multidimensional analysis made possible by the integrated data in the data warehouse and the data analysis and presentation capability offered by BI tools. Multidimensional analysis allows the user to see the data the way he or she uses them.

The end-user component refers to the various user communities that use the data warehouse, as demonstrated in Figure 12.3. The majority of users will be using the static reports most of the time. There is usually a sizeable group of users that will need to look beyond the reports to get the answers they want. They need to drill down or roll up. They need to look at the number from different dimensions. Toward the top of the user pyramid, there are users who need to use advanced data-analysis techniques, such as data mining and longitudinal analysis.

These needs can be addressed by a data warehouse system because of its data content and the special data structure it employs. The data warehouse system not only has to provide different types of access to

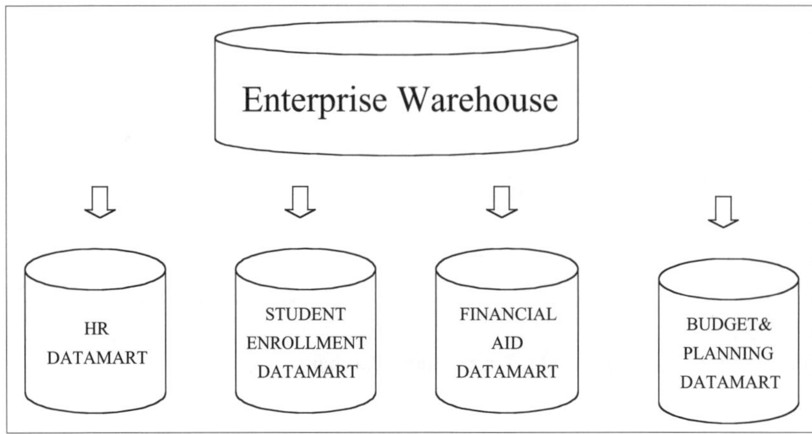

Figure 12.3 Data Warehouse and Data Marts

meet the different information needs, but it also has to provide correct data. This implies that end-users have a very critical role to play in the construction of data warehouses. They should help in selecting source systems and should certainly be involved in designing rules in the data acquisition process that transfers the source data into the data warehouse.

Institutional Support for Data Management

Massy and Wilger suggest that there are three levels of information technology adoption in the teaching and learning process. These stages may have considerable relevance for the adoption of technology to support institutional decision making. Each stage represents "different levels or degrees of innovation" (Massy and Wilger, 1998, p. 50). The levels include:

- Personal productivity aids. This level denotes the use of a standard mode of instruction but "allows teachers and learners to perform familiar tasks faster and more effectively using productivity software for work processing, spreadsheets, and graphing programs."
- Enrichment add-ins. This level adds "new materials to the teaching and learning mix without changing the basic

mode of instruction." This includes the use of e-mail communication and listservs, Web pages, Web search engines, video, and the use of multimedia.

- Paradigm shift. This level is reached when "faculty and their institutions reconfigure teaching and learning activities to take full advantage of the new technology."

Massey and Wilger further suggest that the use of technology and the various levels of technology implementation have implications for quality improvement, productivity gains, and enhanced flexibility and may be a source of cost containment.

In higher education this model has implications for the various levels of investment and commitment to data management and decision-support systems made by institutions. For example, institutions that embrace the practice of data warehousing or institutional data management systems probably have done so in response to internal and external requirements for improved, timely, accurate, and shared information. The commitment to invest in such technology and practice requires tremendous financial and human resources, as well as management investment, and requires a true "paradigm shift" in the way an institution captures, collects, stores, and reports information. Conversely, those institutions unwilling to support an enterprisewide knowledge management solution may simply be content to invest in desktop or "personal productivity" solutions for information and analyses. Consequently, organizational leaders may receive information needed to "get by," while a tremendous amount of flexibility and data richness will be lost. What is needed in developing effective information support for institutional decision making is a paradigm shift that reconceptualizes information systems as critical to decision making. Data warehousing provides an effective means for managing massive amounts of information intended for decision support.

References

Birnbaum, R. (1988). *How colleges work: The cybernetics of academic organizations and leadership*. San Francisco: Jossey-Bass.

Gray, P., and Watson, H. (1998). *Decision support in the data warehouse.* Upper Saddle, NJ: Prentice-Hall.

Hey, D. V. (2000). "Having It All," *Personnel Management,* Vol. 45, (3):127–131.

Inmon, W. H. (1996). *Building the data warehouse.* New York: John Wiley and Sons, Inc.

Kimball, R. (1996). *The data warehouse toolkit: Practical techniques for building dimensional data warehouses.* New York: John Wiley and Sons, Inc.

Linthicum, D. (2000). *Enterprise application integration.* Reading, MA: Addison-Wesley.

Massy, W. F., and Wilger, A. K. (1998). "Technology's contribution to higher education productivity." *New Directions for Higher Education,* 26(3): 49–59.

Soh, C., Kien, S. S., Tay-Yap, J. (2000) "Cultural Fits and Misfits: Is ERP A Universal Solution?" *Communications of the ACM,* vol. 43, No. 4:47–51.

Part 3

Technical or Integrative Best Practices

In this section, you'll read about projects that use technology to provide services to the campus that aren't strictly academic or administrative and may not even be computer-related. For example, Chapter 14, on using voice-over IP, demonstrates the feasibility of using existing computer network wiring to upgrade a phone system without additional wiring costs. The result was an expandable phone system and a network system with more outside connectivity than ever before without breaking the bank.

In Chapter 13, another hot topic in campus information technology is highlighted: the ability to link together unrelated systems to provide single logins and access to multiple databases or sources of information without having to authenticate to several different systems. At Johnson County Community College they designed a portal to provide access to their Internet portal (Campus Pipeline), their course delivery system (Web CT), and their administrative computing system (Banner). Students get one login that shows their distance education courses, on-campus courses, student schedule, bills, financial aid, etc. One of the key advantages of a Web-based system like this is that it can bring together disparate systems that formerly didn't talk to one another by having all of them communicate through Web scripting.

CHAPTER 13

Integrating Learning and Transactional Systems

Del Lovitt, Senior Data Integration Analyst, and Dennis V. Day, Dean of Student Services, Johnson County Community College

Johnson County Community College (JCCC) is in Overland Park, Kansas, 15 miles southwest of downtown Kansas City, Missouri. As a comprehensive community college it offers 60 career programs along with a transfer curriculum that 50 percent of the students take on their way to earning bachelor's degrees at more than 200 universities in the United States and Canada. Enrolling 18,000 students in credit classes each semester and another 20,000 in continuing education programs demands services to be provided efficiently and within growing budget constraints. The average yearly enrollment growth rate for the campus has been 2 percent per year since 1984. A member of the League of Innovation for Community Colleges, JCCC was named one of the top 10 community colleges in North America by a report on community colleges conducted through the University of Texas.

There have been various applications of the term "one stop" in association with higher education. Many colleges and universities have tried to make their recruitment and admission processes one stops to strengthen the image presented to new students and to simplify the contact system. Some have applied the one-stop concept to the registration and payment process, and some have even created one-stop academic support areas where students seek help in all sorts of educational content areas. One stop now has a new meaning for e-learning. Products have been introduced to provide electronic methods of classroom delivery along with content references and access to data in a more selective process than has previously been seen in higher education. Allowing the flexibility to explore these many methods, products, and possibilities has led to a quandary for institutional services. How do you support these somewhat related products, how do you pay for the software and hardware needed to provide required platforms, and who will need to be familiar with all of these possibilities? More importantly, how can we provide a one view (stop) of these divergent but related products to our users? We want to simplify their access; we want to create an experience that provides "no stops" to their educational pursuits.

At Johnson County Community College 12 percent of the 18,000 credit students were enrolled in distance delivery courses and another 25 percent in classes where supplemental materials are offered via the Internet in 2002 and 2003. To support these courses a growing selection of products are used and the need for expanding support has become critical. When working with creative people, such as content faculty, limits are not always embraced particularly in a research setting or where it is critical to be progressive and keep up with students' learning needs (or delivery needs). JCCC's distance learning course enrollments are growing at a rate of 25 percent each year since 1999 and have leaped from the last choice during enrollment to the first choice of students beginning in 2002. Students are busy; they are not just students in our setting but are making choices that fit their specific lifestyles. "You mean I can stay at work and take a course, or I can stay at home and do the research and not go to the library on campus?" These are familiar refrains in the new millennium.

Distance learning (and the use of classroom supplemental material via the Internet) is not going away; it is slowly becoming ingrained into the societal reality as an acceptable choice rather than the unique item in educational journals. The promise of the delivery system now has to be met. Instructors and students need access to Internet-based systems; materials must be in a readable and easily updateable format. Technical support must be in place to assist those who encounter problems at home, on campus, at work, or in a coffee shop downtown. Providing both human and material resources became a constant concern to JCCC as the number of students wanting this option increased. To ensure each instructor and student had the access they needed, materials in the format they desired, and the support they required, something had to be done to consolidate the demand on resources.

Where Do We Start?

Web-based products have been available for 10 years since the early 1990s, but at that time there were pioneers who were adventurous while exploring the uses of the Internet. Those pioneers began experimenting with supplemental materials, such as virtual tours of the Parthenon for a humanities class or copies of text not found in the library but posted on the Internet by some resourceful agency or individual to assist in a political science course. Our appetites were whetted with CU-SeeMe technology and the introduction of chat room conversations. As exploration in various Internet-based products continued, the demand for more money and more support caused resources to be stretched too thin to satisfy all requests. Administrators and instructional leaders gathered to address the impending decisions that loomed as the e-world evolved.

Issues concerning student and employee records, registration, and direct communication with students were more easily answered since this impacted the administrative mechanism of the college rather than the instructional units. Web registration, Internet-delivered applications, and electronic access to records were developed and provided by software companies. One such product is Campus Pipeline, which allowed the administrative functions and student transactions to be consolidated through a Web portal system. This portal provided authenticated access to data once restricted to the user, as well as a unified authentication process for various transactions once done manually by offices throughout the college campus or by the administrative software used by JCCC since 1995.

Course delivery for distance learning was evaluated using various Internet-based products throughout the early 1990s. Several solutions were proposed to the college as Internet service expanded into households in the service area. In Fall 2000, JCCC settled on WEB CT as the preferred provider of Web-based courses and content material. This decision, while made and supported by instructional representatives, was a result of experimentation and research on the available e-learning delivery systems of the time.

At this juncture, SCT Banner (the administrative software), Campus Pipeline (a Web portal system) and WEB CT (a content-delivery system) were functioning as separate components but were pulled together at various points when data needed to be shared through structured query language (sql) scripts, shared data files, or just through the sheer determination of an individual. Sharing student-related data with systems was becoming more challenging. While answers had been provided to consolidate data records, Web services, and course delivery systems there was still a need to bring these three main systems together in a seamless self-service model to students, faculty, and staff.

The information services (technology) staff gathered to identify strategic goals for the institution that would integrate these systems for JCCC. The continued usage of the home-grown integrated system was a major linchpin in the decision-making process. The current operating system shared a database allowing data to be entered in different applications and shared by other applications through interfaces. Rather than create or develop a new homegrown system, a strategic decision was made to purchase a compatible solution. Even though there were enough talented resources on staff to develop a solution, their particular talents were committed to other projects. Another decision-making factor involved time: demand for application development in other areas on campus and the time to develop a new system would delay implementation. Relying on the creativity and software development of a major corporate provider seemed to be the correct strategy so the institution could get past the questions stage and get right into the answers stage. Other objectives for the purchased system were to provide a single sign-on for users with all the integrated applications, improve self-service for all constituents, and to eliminate, where possible, back-end processing. This "Connected Learning Solution" was considered a high priority and resources were made available to move this project along.

The desire to offer to students a one-stop-shopping image of the college from recruitment visuals, to articulation transcripts, to purchases of text and materials, to course delivery, and support services was growing throughout our service areas. Taking a course on demand, just as one might order an on-demand movie or a take-out meal, was driving the marketplace. This is not to diminish the value of the course, but it is a vivid image of the "new" student enrolled in several different schools to get what they want when they want it.

The Plan

The formation of the implementation team took careful planning and consideration based on the defined goals and a clear understanding of project scope as it crossed functional and technical support areas of the organization. It required members from a variety of areas within information services, as these systems were being administered in different divisions (see Figure 13.1). Finally, the selected team members included:

- Project Leader
- WebCT Technical Lead
- Connected Learning Solutions Technical Lead
- Campus Pipeline Technical Lead
- Oracle/Banner Data Base Administrator
- Director of Academic Computing Services
- Director of Administrative Computing Services
- Chief Information Officer

Once the team defined the project goals and scope, the roles and specific responsibilities were matched with various milestones. Some of these include using XML batch file imports to initially build the u-portal and course content systems, transaction-based data synchronization to keep data current, and functionality for a single authentication process to be used to acquire information specific to

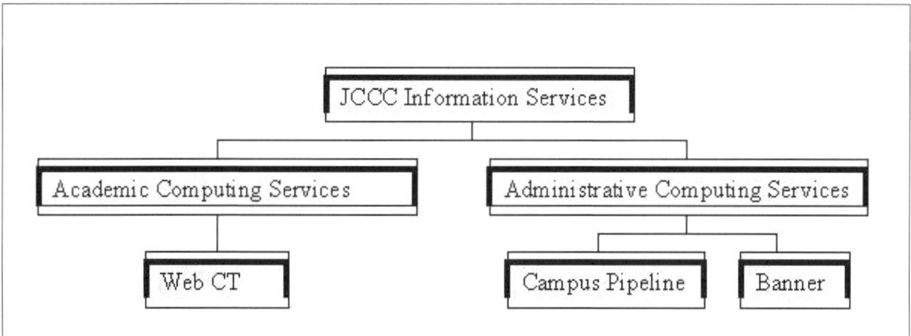

Figure 13.1 Information Service Flow Chart

the constituent from any of the systems. For each of the systems there was an identified system administrator responsible for the installation and maintenance tasks and issues. The project lead acted as a liaison between the functional and technical areas while leading the implementation team with tasks to successfully deploy the project on time. As additional issues were encountered in the process, there were decision makers on the team to help provide solutions to issues specific to the organization. With regularly scheduled implementation meetings, expectations for communication amongst team members and terminology differences in the products were identified up front as items to be addressed. In addition to using standard project management methodologies in completing the implementation, testing, and deployment phases, there was a collaborative effort with the team members to identify and address any potential issues pertaining to the request.

Organizational Climate and Business Practices

This team actively participates in the support of the technology used to perform many of the daily business processes on campus, but there was a gap in understanding the relevance and importance to performing these processes. Time was dedicated to educating the team members on the reasons for using these procedures and the impact integration of these systems would have on the processes. Enrollment schedules, student drop processes, faculty assignments, and building course schedules were among some of the business processes targeted. This level of detail escalated the level of awareness for the importance of data integration among these systems to improve processes.

As with any campuswide project, issues are identified throughout the planning and implementation processes. However, in this effort the issues were not only project-related but also organizational. For example, the integration of these systems highlighted two issues with the existing organization: customer support contacts for the various populations of students, faculty, and staff were different. In order to provide a seamless self-service model using the one-stop shopping model, interaction with customers needed to be more consistent and centralized to efficiently handle requests and dispatch services to them. Also, communication methods were not consistent and occurred at random intervals throughout the semester for information services staff, the campuswide functional areas, and the outside community accessing the college's resources. When significant changes impacted these groups, developing a communication procedure would reduce the level of anxiety and concerns. Although these issues existed long before the integration of systems, they were more pronounced with the integration. One of the outcomes of this project will be to evaluate the best practices for these issues considering the technological enhancements. As a result, a cross-functional team has been assigned to look at the vision of these services and implement a standard communication plan for future requests.

As illustrated in Figure 13.2 the target for this project was to link an administrative database (Banner), a Web portal (Campus Pipeline), and a course delivery system (Web CT) together for greater functionality and ease of authentication by the user. An integrated solution was planned by the team to bring a personalized access point for the user. This entry point created a visual integration of the different applications available, ensuring that the data was shared as authentication occurred. Multiple constituencies were considered as the solutions were designed, personalized based on the user's role and function. Therefore, this solution considered the types of access needed to secure information based on the constituent and relationship to the organization. For example, students are able to view transcripts, register, make payments, perform degree audits, and access e-mail. Faculty can enter grades, view rosters, conduct chats and threaded discussions, and access e-mail.

The deployment of this request was completed and the beginning of implementation tasks started by March 2003. In relation to proposed and delivered timelines, there were approximate dates assigned as "go-live" dates, which were contingent on the success of previous steps in the process. As expected, there were issues such as basic hardware configuration settings needing to be fine-tuned for system environments, application defects required patches from vendors, and the need to clarify data import for optimal system integration. These and other issues required the project team to identify resolutions in order to proceed. Undoubtedly each of these examples provided learning opportunities for the implementation team to better understand the integration between systems technically and functionally, as well as find methods to troubleshoot issues and develop standard checklists before contacting the vendor for support. Upon final testing, the

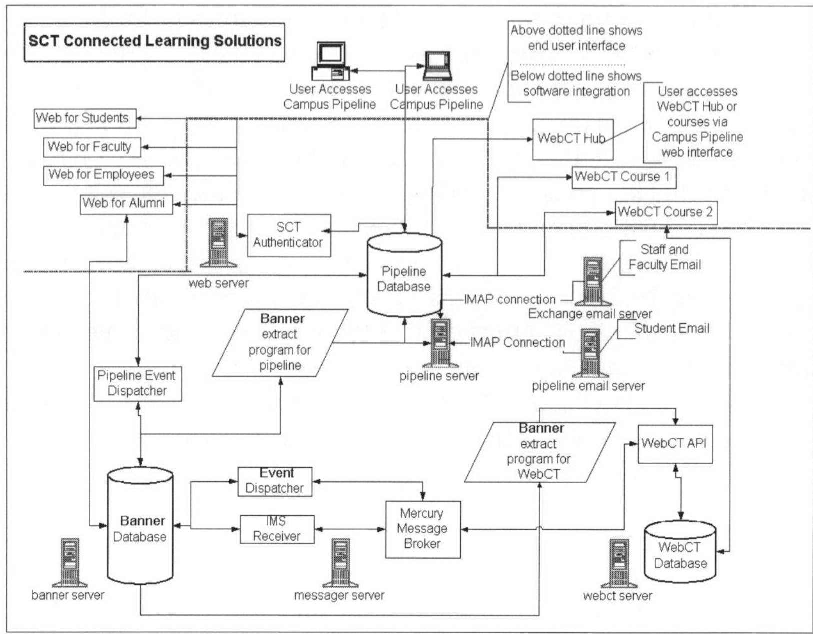

Figure 13.2 SCT Connected Learning Solutions

request was completed and deployed by July 1, 2003, for the remainder of the summer term activity and the onslaught of fall.

Results

Some of the outcomes for this project include the evaluation of best practices for customer support, the implementation of standard communication strategies, and the coordination of a cross-functional team for future planning of upgrades to the systems. With these efforts underway, the integration of systems, support, and communication become new goals for the organization. To make changes in processes and systems now impacts the entire campus given the integration that has occurred. Therefore, we are learning to communicate more effectively and prepare more strategically for future enhancements and initiatives.

Specific changes that have occurred as a result of this integration have been:

- Service or "help desk" resources have been consolidated and require only one telephone call or one e-mail request. These are routed to service personnel without the user having to decide who should be notified (i.e., regardless of whether the requestor is a student, faculty member, or staff person).

- Notices and alerts are now routed through the software and can be set up as specific e-mail messages directed at individuals or as announcements to all or selected populations.

- Data is entered into the administrative system and shared by all segments of the "connected learning chain."

As a result of these changes, we now must evaluate the effectiveness and the utility of the project. Surveys of the student and staff population are being prepared to assess the access to support systems and the communications about the use of the software systems. Data from these surveys will assist in enhancements to the operations and the uses of the "connected learning systems." Fiscal outcomes will be monitored to determine if there will be efficiencies gained as the disparate systems are integrated. An audit of the systems and operational costs should determine if the synergies created through this weaving of software produces an economy of effort, administrative control, and IT value.

On a college campus, any project that brings together administrative and instructional priorities for the good of the institution is valuable. This project is one of those win-win initiatives that is benefiting all populations and preparing the campus for the next level of e-learning.

CHAPTER 14

Implementing Campuswide Voice-Over Internet Protocol (VoIP) Phone Systems at a Small College

Nichole Howa Greenwood, Telecommunications Coordinator and Stephan Ross, Computer Support Manager/Webmaster, Information Technology Department Westminster College

Introduction

Founded in 1875 as the Salt Lake Collegiate Institute, Westminster College is a private, independent college offering professional and liberal arts courses of study as well as selected graduate programs. We are dedicated to the integration of liberal arts with career and professional education in a learning environment that is supportive and challenging. Our programs build on the experiences students bring to the college in order to prepare them further for lives of learning, accomplishment, and service. The college emphasizes excellence in teaching and personalized instruction and provides support services to meet the needs of students of diverse ages and backgrounds.

The Westminster College campus is situated in a residential area of Salt Lake City within the shadows of the Wasatch Mountains. There are approximately 115 full-time faculty and 140 associate instructors who teach at Westminster College. Westminster has a combination of approximately 2,400 full-time and part-time students. Seventy-eight percent are undergraduate students, 22 percent are graduate students. Students are offered a choice of 30 undergraduate programs and majors as well as graduate degrees in business administration, education, professional communication, and nursing.

Project Scope

The Westminster Information Technology (IT) department replaced an outdated, traditional Private Branch Exchange (PBX) NEC MMG phone system for the campus during May–June 2001 with a state-of-the-art Voice-Over Internet Protocol (VoIP) system.

In 1997 Westminster received a 15-year-old NEC MMG phone system as a donation from a local company to replace our aging NEC system. The donated phone system became problematic over time: It was running at full capacity and could not accommodate the addition of new buildings, required frequent troubleshooting and repair, had significant heat damage, and was fast becoming antiquated. With the advent of VoIP technologies, the IT staff did a comparative cost-benefit analysis and review of VoIP vs. traditional phone systems over a 12-month period. Despite our initial reluctance at adopting a relatively new technology, VoIP emerged as the clear winner.

We worked with our vendor, Consonus, and with Cisco Systems directly to determine the types of equipment needed to support our current data network. Once we had developed a project strategy we determined an initial six month timeline to implement both the voice and voice-mail systems, upgrade our data systems, and train our users. However, we found that the installation took only two months because everything went so smoothly.

Implementation of the VoIP Voice/Voice-Mail Systems and Upgrade to Westminster's Data Systems

Implementation of the new technology was relatively straightforward. We successfully implemented a full Cisco Avvid VoIP system including new servers, switches, routers, phone hardware, and a robust voice-mail system, and upgraded our existing data network in two months. We installed new powered switches in every closet so the power for the phone was transmitted from one location instead of from each individual phone. We moved from a 10 megabit backbone to a 100 megabit backbone, and we introduced redundancy at the core switches and routers. During the project we ran into a few difficulties with the connections between the traditional PBX and the Cisco Avvid VoIP system, which caused us to work more aggressively in order to meet our deadline. The final installation process was completed at the end of June 2001.

New Campus Number Convention

The number changeover was relatively simple. We worked with the Web interface to program all phones, gateways, numbers, calling patterns, and Primary Rate Interface (PRI) connections. We encountered some major problems with the voice-mail system: message indicators would not turn on, voice-mail boxes would lock users out, the entire system would stop running and we would have to reboot it at least once a week, we could not mass-download a large group of users, and we could not completely delete users. Our solution was to completely rebuild the voice-mail server from scratch, adding each extension individually, and it has since been stable.

End-User Training

We provided training for the new phones and voice-mail system for faculty and staff; residence hall students were not trained but picked up the new technology with no difficulties. IT staff provided training in groups to help with the different types of phones that each person would be using. Faculty and students received a single-line phone and staff received a six-line phone. The training sessions were held according to when each office would be switching from the old system to the new system. The training was held in a hands-on environment so that two people were able to share one phone and become comfortable with the phone interface, placing calls on hold, transferring calls, setting up voice mail, and retrieving voice-mail messages.

Legacy Phone System, Cabling, and Analog Lines

Our vendor, Consonus, took our old phone system donated from OC Tanner as well as the original NEC system as a trade-in. All of our existing cabling for telecommunications was left in place, and we have abandoned most of it with the exceptions of a few fax lines. We did add analog service to our existing VoIP system by installing a data card into our router that converts digital signal to analog signal; we use these analog lines for our emergency and elevator phones.

Project Team

The VoIP project team consisted of three IT staff, one Value-Added Reseller (VAR), and the VoIP hardware vendor. Additional IT staff assisted as needed.

Nichole Howa Greenwood, telecommunications coordinator, was tasked with administering the VoIP system.

Robert Allred, network and administrative database manager, took on the role of project leader.

Collin Bunker served as data network administrator.

Consonus acted in an advisory capacity and provided on-site technical support.

CISCO Systems, the VoIP system vendor, also provided on-site technical support.

Project Budget

The initial bid for this project came in at $1 million. When we made the decision about the two finalists, the bids came in much lower at around $650,000. We made our final decision to go with the Cisco VoIP system and found we had to add a few more items to complete the system, bringing our final price for the project to about $750,000.

Who Benefited?

Westminster faculty, staff, and students benefited greatly from this project. More than 1,000 phones were installed and are currently running; we also increased overall data backbone capacity and reliability.

Conclusion

Initially we did not feel that a VoIP solution was worth considering because the technology was still so new, and there had not at that time been an installation of a VoIP system as large as ours would need to be. Once we started looking into the idea of VoIP and toured a few locations to see what they had done with it, we saw it as a sound and robust solution.

The installation proceeded more smoothly and quickly than we had anticipated, but we did run into a problem connecting the old system to the new system and feel that we should have done more to ensure it would be stable and usable. We found that the two systems did not like to communicate with each other; we lost the ability to transfer calls from the old system to the new system, yet we could transfer the opposite way. We also found that the number of outgoing calls from both systems working together was limited to about 22–23 calls at one time because one system had to use the other to make a connection to the Public Switched Telephone Network (PSTN). This caused the circuits to busy out, and would not allow for incoming, outgoing, or Direct Inward Dial (DID) calls to be made.

In hindsight, we now know that we could have added more PRI/T1 interface connections to allow for more calls to be placed and received. There is nothing that we could have done to assist with the functionality of the two systems communicating with each other. There were a few problems that were unexpected by both Westminster College and our Cisco/Consonus team members, but there was nothing that could not be resolved.

The most critical point is that any institution implementing VoIP should do as much of the installation and setup work as possible rather than having it done by a consultant or the vendor. The staff, which will be working on the system after the installation, should perform the actual installation. The bottom line is to make sure you have help, but to do the work yourselves so that you are thoroughly knowledgeable with the system.

We view the VoIP project as a strong success. The following are key areas for evaluation:

Expandability: Hardware and bandwidth permitting, we can add a limitless number of phones and phone configurations to the VoIP system.

Stability: The system continues to perform stably and consistently.

Integration: The data and voice systems work hand-in-hand with one another. If we upgrade one system the other is upgraded as well. The two separate budget lines for data and voice have now been combined so that we have only one account. We have seen a huge savings in maintenance and repair and have extra money to spend on new and upcoming technology that will also integrate with our current network, i.e., wireless technologies.

CHAPTER 15

Administration of Information Technology at a Small Liberal Arts University

Ronnie Swanner, Director and
Pat Ullmann, Production Manager
Trinity University

Overview

In the spring of 2000 the administrative structure at Trinity University was changed to add a vice-presidential-level position for information technology. Prior to that time, most IT directors reported to the Vice-President for Academic Affairs or to an Associate Vice-President for Academic Affairs. Concurrent with the creation of the new office, all of Trinity's IT departments, some of which previously had been sub-departments under other administrative entities, were given equal status and placed directly under the new Vice-President. These changes were made in part to recognize the increased level of importance that IT was playing in the university and to provide a more effective voice for technology on campus.

To set the context for a discussion of the evolution of IT administrative structure on our campus, it seems appropriate to provide some background regarding the university and a brief description of our IT facilities.

Trinity University is a small, private liberal arts and sciences institution located in San Antonio, Texas. We are primarily undergraduate and primarily residential. Our enrollment averages around 2700. Our class size averages seventeen, and our instructor-to-student ratio is about 1:11. The majority of our faculty appointments are full-time, permanent, tenure-track positions. Ninety-nine percent of our 210 full-time academic faculty members hold a Ph.D. degree or terminal degree in their field. Trinity consistently ranks at or near the top among our peer institutions in nationally recognized surveys of colleges and universities. We are governed by a Board of Trustees, and our senior administration consists of the university President and five Vice-Presidents.

Trinity University operates three general computing labs on campus, providing a total of eighty-three Windows-based stations. These labs provide basic office-suite software and network/internet connectivity, as well as the occasional specialized software application when requested by an instructor in connection with a specific class. In addition to the general labs, there are a handful of small labs on campus that provide higher-end or specialized software and hardware for individual departments or specific purposes such as digital video editing.

For classroom instruction involving the use of digital or other media material, Trinity operates 53 electronic classrooms offering varying degrees of equipment sophistication. These classrooms will be discussed in detail in a later section.

All campus providers of computer and other information technology and technology support services at Trinity report to the office of the Vice-President for Information Resources and Administrative Affairs (VPIRAA), a relatively new office created in an administrative reorganization in 2000. The technology-related units under the VPIRAA include the university Library; Information Technology Services (the campus computer center); Instructional Media Services (the campus media center); and the TigerCard office (which administers the campuswide swipe-card system). A brief description of each of these units follows.

Elizabeth Huth Coates Library

The Coates Library is a fine undergraduate research library housing a collection of one million books and bound periodicals. The library provides several dedicated computer stations for various types of online information retrieval, and until 2003 it also housed a 35-station general computer lab. This traditional, compartmentalized lab was done away with in the summer of 2003 as part of the Information Commons project, discussed in detail later, which is designed around a new concept of the integration of technology and digital resources with a traditional library setting. Also relatively new to the library (introduced in 2001) is Java City, a coffee/snack bar on the main floor of the building, which was expanded in the summer of 2003 to become an integral part of the new "village commons" atmosphere of gathering, learning, and sharing information in an open, interactive space that was a major goal of the Information Commons project.

Information Technology Services (ITS)

This department is responsible for the installation, configuration, administration, and maintenance of the campus LAN and of all general computing labs, faculty/staff computers, and classroom computers. In addition, ITS assists students in configuring their own computers in the dorms; provides individual user support for students, faculty, and staff for a wide variety of hardware and software; repairs and maintains all computer-related hardware and peripherals on campus; and administers all site-licensed software.

Instructional Media Services (IMS)

IMS is responsible for the delivery and setup of all media-related equipment on campus; for design, implementation and installation, maintenance, and user support for all electronic classrooms; for the production of media materials (digital images, slides, prints, CDs/DVDs, videorecordings, etc.) for use in classroom instruction or faculty research; and for the repair and maintenance of all campus audiovisual equipment. In addition, IMS operates a small high-end computer lab, the Multimedia Development Center, offering digital production capabilities and multiple-platform access not found in the campus general computer labs. IMS is responsible as well for the video and audio conferencing facilities on campus and for the university's video streaming capabilities.

In addition, IMS maintains and operates the hardware and distribution system for the campus cable television service, which carries Time-Warner cable programming as well as two local closed-circuit channels originated by Trinity. The first local channel, TigerTV, is managed by students and broadcasts student-created programming as well as a selection of feature films supplied by Swank, Inc., a contract provider of motion picture content to educational institutions. The second campus channel is generated and managed by IMS and provides a program guide for TigerTV as well as TigerTV movie previews and general campus information. IMS oversees the contracts with both Time Warner and Swank. The campus cable TV service is supplied to all classrooms, dorm rooms and TV lounges, and to selected other rooms and offices.

In the fall of 2002, software training for faculty and staff was added to the services provided by IMS. The position of Instructional Support Manager was created in IMS to provide training in office productivity and course-management software (more on this function follows in the "Initiatives" section).

TigerCard Office

In 2002, Trinity introduced a swipe-card system designed to combine in one card the functions of ID card, library card, access card for electronically controlled building entry, and debit card for many university services. Students or their parents place a sum of money on the card, and those dollars, called TigerBucks, are then electronically deducted from the card when it is swiped at any campus point-of-service. The TigerCard office was established to oversee this system, with its first major responsibility being the Pharos pay-for-print service placed in the campus computer labs in the fall semester of 2002. Pay-services on the card were phased in over a period of several months. At present (Spring 2004) students are able to use their TigerCards for meals, laundry, vending machines, computer printers, copy machines, and other similar services on campus; and students and administrators have begun to discuss the possibility of the university entering into agreements with some nearby off-campus establishments such as grocery or convenience stores that would enable TigerBucks to be accepted at those stores as well.

As will be apparent from these summaries, there are several areas in which these four departments overlap. At Trinity as elsewhere, many of the distinctions that once existed between the duties of librarians, media technicians, and computing support providers are disappearing or being redefined. IMS staff, for example, frequently troubleshoot computer-related problems in classrooms, and ITS staff install and maintain the printers and release stations for the Pharos system. The staff and supervisors of all four areas need to work closely together and share information on an on-going basis. Until our reorganization, however, administrative oversight of these units was divided, and often there was little or no high-level coordination between them. The office of Vice-President for Information Resources and Administrative Affairs was created in 2000 to bring these areas together under one administrative umbrella and to create both short-term goals and long-term vision for information technology at Trinity. All four units described here (as well as the Registrar and the Office of Conferences & Special Programs) now report directly to the VPIRAA.

Initiatives

In addition to administratively unifying all technology-related services at Trinity, the new Vice-Presidential office also is charged with ensuring that our institution remains on the cutting edge in terms of the instructional and information technology that we can offer to our students and faculty. As we move into the 21st century this has become a critical measure of a university's quality, and keeping up with it is a challenging responsibility in an era of continuous innovation, changing technologies and multiple standards. Since the creation of the office in 2000, the first and current VPIRAA, Dr. Charles White, has spearheaded several technology-related initiatives at Trinity. The most important among these are briefly discussed here.

Information Commons

The name 'Information Commons' was carefully chosen for Trinity's most ambitious technology-related project in recent years. Many meanings of the word 'common' can be read into the choice: among others, the Oxford English Dictionary offers "belonging to all mankind alike"; "of or belonging to the community at large"; and "free to be used by everyone, public;" all of which in a university context are applicable to knowledge in the broadest and highest sense. In addition, the name suggests a descendant of the "village commons" of earlier times, and Trinity's Information Commons serves a parallel function for our academic community: a central space that is available for all members of the community to use in pursuit of their common goals of learning, teaching, and collaborating.

The Information Commons provides a variety of computer hardware, software, and peripherals, and offers both hardwired and wireless LAN and Internet access. Power and data ports are available for users to connect their own personal laptops. The area features comfortable furniture and lighting arranged in several different configurations, including areas for group work and smaller spaces for individual research. The Commons floor is open and visually inviting, with few walls, few stacks, and many windows. Reference librarians and technology experts together staff a central Help Desk, assisting Trinity students and professors in accessing and synthesizing information and preparing it for presentation or publication. These professionals emphasize information literacy and critical thinking skills as they work with students to locate and evaluate scholarly information. In addition, the university contracted with Kinko's to incorporate a storefront in the Commons, providing copying, faxing, scanning, and printing services to students, faculty, and staff. TigerBucks are accepted at this in-house Kinko's.

The Information Commons also houses a small high-tech classroom that does duty both as an instructional facility for general computing topics, and as a Geographical Information Systems (GIS) training room. GIS is a rapidly-expanding technology (or suite of technologies) for using computer processing power to analyze, interpret and synthesize geographically oriented data from a wide variety of sources, such as topographic maps, census data and political surveys. GIS software combines geographic and demographic data with visualization tools, and can be used in every discipline from business to communications, from sociology to geology. The GIS training room will provide a computer at each student seat, and will be fully equipped as one of our highest-level electronic classrooms.

The Information Commons can be used by individuals working on their own, but it is intended also to promote the gathering and working together of members of the university community in an atmosphere that is part academic, part social. The Commons project incorporated an expanded version of the pre-existing Java City coffee shop, another initiative of the current VPIRAA that has been an enormous success with our student body. As discussed below, the coffee shop has helped to create a new image of the library as a friendly place for students to congregate and work, and it meshes seamlessly with the ambience of the Information Commons.

Wireless Network Access and Laptop Checkout

In the summer of 2002, a wireless network pilot program was instituted in the Trinity library. Wireless receivers, or access points, were ceiling mounted throughout the building, covering all four floors. The university then purchased 25 laptop computers, configured them with wireless network cards, and made them available for student checkout at the IMS circulation desk. (Students also have the option of purchasing a wireless network card for their own laptops at the campus bookstore.) Logging on via the wireless network in the library accesses the campus LAN in the same way that logging on to any conventional wired computer on campus does. The coverage area extends a limited distance outside the library building, allowing students sitting at picnic tables or on the lawn in front of the building to work on their computers with full network access.

This pilot program was and is a huge success, with the checkout laptops in constant demand. During the ensuing year (2002–2003), we expanded wireless coverage to include all of the academic buildings and selected common areas in the residence halls. When total coverage of the residence halls is completed, we will be able to offer wireless network access to our students and faculty from anywhere on campus.

Blackboard

In the summer of 2000 Trinity University purchased its first license for a course-management software package, Blackboard. After an extensive investigation of the available software packages, Blackboard was selected because of its robustness and ease of use. Faculty were not required to use Blackboard but were encouraged to do so by training sessions explaining the features and benefits of the system. That fall, 25 courses were Blackboard-enabled, meaning that some level of use was made of Blackboard in that class. In 2001 Trinity upgraded the Blackboard software, purchased an enterprise license and implemented our portal. In the fall semester of 2002, 270 classes were Blackboard-enabled. Many courses are now heavily dependent on Blackboard to provide additional course content, group chat, and class e-mail messages, information that would not be part of regular classroom instruction.

In the fall of 2003, Trinity began offering faculty the option of using a competing product, WebCT, for Web-based course management. This decision was reached after re-evaluating the cost and features available with the current course-management software versions. Based on cost versus features for each package, we felt that WebCT had supplanted Blackboard as the best system for our use. However, our administration did not want to force the faculty to convert to WebCT, as there is no easy, automated way to make that transition. Content in Blackboard must be manually re-entered in WebCT. Instead of forcing faculty to switch, it was thought that providing both systems would allow professors the opportunity to try both and to decide for themselves which package offered them the most benefit and the greatest comfort level. During the spring of 2004, faculty use of each package is being evaluated, and a decision soon will be reached as to whether we should continue to support both packages or should standardize on one or the other.

Instructional Support Manager Position

In 2002, the VPIRAA was instrumental in creating a new full-time position, that of Instructional Support Manager, in the department of Instructional Media Services. The incumbent of this position provides instruction, in a small group setting or one-on-one, for faculty and staff in the use of various software applications such as office productivity and graphics imaging packages. In addition, the Instructional Support Manger conducts training sessions for Blackboard and WebCT users, and maintains the department's Web site.

Java City

One of the more innovative ideas implemented by the VPIRAA, the Java City Coffee Shop has fundamentally altered the face of the academic library at Trinity. The coffee shop was conceived as one response to a challenge faced not just by Trinity but by academic libraries across the country: In an age when information that was once exclusively housed in library collections has become available at the click of a key from the comfort of home, how does the institution of the library remain relevant? Ironically, the reality is that the library and its professional staff are as important as ever, if not more so, in this era of information overload: students need assistance in locating, accessing, and winnowing information, and guidance in evaluating it. But library door counts are dropping nationwide, and information literacy among students is becoming questionable at best. Too many students simply do a Google search on a research topic and use the first ten results that pop up.

Trinity, like several other institutions in the U.S., has responded by trying to make the library a more friendly and inviting place. The coffee shop, which opened for business in the fall of 2001, is a cornerstone of a new concept of the library as meeting area, group study hall, and pleasant place to relax between classes. The hope is that students who might otherwise study or do research in their dorm rooms will instead choose to come to the library, and once there will avail themselves of our information and services.

Pharos Pay-for-Print System

Until the summer of 2002, Trinity University provided free black-and-white laser printing for students using the campus computer labs and library research stations. As the use of online resources and electronic instructional materials burgeoned, however, the cost to the university of providing this service became prohibitive. Because printing was free there was no incentive for students to be selective in what they printed, and there was an enormous amount of wastage. The solution for which Trinity opted was a system called Pharos Uni-Print, which charges computer users for the hard copy they print. Students use TigerCards to pay for prints at Pharos swipe-card stations located in each computer lab on campus. Currently, the university gives each student 125 free prints each semester; beyond that number, black-and-white laser prints cost $.09 each, while color laser prints are $.75. It is Trinity's hope that this system will not only allow the university to recover some of the cost of operating the printers, but also will encourage resource conservation by giving students an incentive to print only what they really need.

Electronic Classrooms

In the summer of 1984 Trinity renovated the largest classroom on campus, the 175-seat Science Lecture Hall, incorporating as much then-current audiovisual technology as possible and creating our first electronic classroom. At that time personal computing was in its infancy and installing a stand-alone computer in the room was not an option. Instead, we installed a computer terminal connected by coaxial cable to the campus mainframe. In addition to displaying on the instructor's monitor, the image from the computer could simultaneously be projected on a nine-foot screen by way of a ceiling mounted CRT data projector. This concept, so commonplace now, was just being accepted for use in classrooms at the time, and Barco, the projector manufacturer, sent a public relations team to campus to produce an article on our implementation.

We have come a long way from that beginning. Today, our 53 electronic classrooms are divided into four basic categories. Level I provides the projected display of video images only, while Level II adds the ability to project computer (data) images as well. Level III adds an instructor's station complete with computer and built-in touch-panel control of the room's AV equipment, including a DVD/VHS player, sound system, slide projector, data projector, input switching system, and computer. (In our most recent configurations, the slide projector is an optional feature, since the use of slides in classroom instruction has dropped significantly. Instead, faculty are increasingly incorporating digital information into their presentations and displaying that information through the data projector.) Level IV, our highest-end electronic classroom, includes all of the previous features and adds a computer for each student, as well as a sophisticated computer control/switching system with which the instructor can control the keyboard, mouse, and monitor of each student, and display the image from any student's computer on the projection screen for the entire class to view. While this level of technology support is not required in most classes, these Level IV classrooms are in high demand by our faculty. We currently operate five of these classrooms.

In general, each year we convert three or four classrooms to electronic classrooms, and simultaneously upgrade the equipment in five or six existing electronic classrooms. However, the current year (2003–2004) saw the completion of a new administration and classroom building, which added six classrooms, one training room, five seminar rooms, and five conference rooms, all equipped with varying levels of electronic support. These additional rooms will significantly increase the level of classroom technology access provided for our faculty and students.

Conclusion

Though we are just ending our fourth year of this administrative structure, it has proven to be very effective and will probably remain in force for the foreseeable future. University-wide evaluations of the VPIRAA conducted in 2003 indicate that the structure is working well from both the administrative and faculty/staff perspective. No administrative change was recommended by the evaluation committees nor anticipated from the administration.

There are probably nearly as many different ways to administer university information technology services as there are universities, but this approach is one that works very well for our institution. This organizational model has made for improved communication between IT departments, a more collegial working atmosphere among departments, and less competition between departments for staff, resources, and budget. Having direct representation, through the new vice-president, to the university president and to other high-level campus administrators has given the division more visibility, emphasized the importance of its role in the university, improved the speed of decision making and allowed the redirection of division staff, resources, and budget in a more efficient and effective manner. Ultimately, the reorganization has helped the IT departments to better serve our clients, the university students, faculty, and staff, which is of course our primary goal.

Part 4

Future Best Practices

The projects described in the following chapters are proposals to solve current problems and address future needs. These "visionaries" have researched and detailed project plans and those plans are discussed within.

"A Model for Monitoring and Migrating Web Resources" envisions a new way to monitor Web usage that makes surfing and locating information from vast resources easier for the user and provides the Web site owner with statistics on who is using which resources while still maintaining anonymity and privacy.

"A Vision of the Internet in 2010" discusses how anytime/anywhere access will be accomplished along with more freedom, sharing of code, and speed to allow virtually any types of applications to be run on the Internet.

Finally, "The One-Room Schoolhouse (Internet Portal) for K-12 Schools" takes a relatively simple concept, that of an Internet-accessible databank, and proposes a solution to help K-12 educators master a continually changing set of educational requirements. Faculty and students of pedagogy or teacher education will be intrigued by the idea of having lesson plans, tutorials, and other resources available at their fingertips in the classroom. The concept itself has applicability to many other areas, not the least of which would be higher education; publicly accessible teaching databanks by subject area could be invaluable resources to both new and experienced teachers.

These authors have taken some risks in trying to predict Web services and applications several years out; in Information Technology, predicting even a year or two out can be difficult. There is little doubt that these resources would change the way we use the Internet, teach, and educate our students.

CHAPTER 16

A Model for Monitoring and Migrating Web Resources

M. P. Evans, Department of Computer Science
University of Reading and
S. M. Furnell, Network Research Group,
Department of Communication and Electronic Engineering
University of Plymouth

Introduction

Web site owners require detailed statistics on the Web resources (e.g., HTML documents, images, Java applets) that their users request. Usually, this information is recorded in a Web server access log, which provides a history of the resources served by the server, and so helps the server owner monitor the usage of a Web site. However, of far more interest to historians, sociologists, and others interested in the changing interests of the online society, would be a system capable of measuring the resource usage of the Web as a whole. Such a system would provide dynamic insights into the changing nature of Web usage, as well as accurate marketing information for the Web site owner, and more effective navigation for the user.

This chapter presents a model for such a system. Although the model is only described, its core architecture is based on a fully tested prototype, which is capable of scaling to many times the size of today's Web (as of April 2004, Google indexed 4,285,199,774 HTML documents) (Google, 2004).

The chapter begins with a brief overview of current techniques for recording resource usage, and their limitations. We then present our system for enabling Web resources to migrate across Web servers transparently, and show how this system can be extended to record resource usage across the Web. Then we discuss the advantages of monitoring Web-wide resource usage by providing examples of new applications that can use the usage information. The chapter ends with a discussion on issues and further work in progress.

Limitations of Existing Monitoring Techniques

Monitoring resource usage is important for Web site owners and advertisers alike, and there are a variety of techniques for providing such a service. However, existing techniques are unsuitable for monitoring usage across the Web.

Web Server Access Logs. The most common technique for recording resource usage is to analyze a Web server access log, which records details about the user's request, the server's response, and the resource that was requested.

Limitations for Web-Wide Monitoring. The information contained in a Web server log is specific to that server only, and is accessible only to the server owner. Capturing Web-wide information is therefore impossible.

Web Bugs. A Web bug is a client-based solution that subverts the HTML *IMG* element to record usage patterns of advertisements (Krishnamurthy and Rexford, 2001). The bug is usually a one-pixel image that is transparent, and so invisible to the end user. It is served by an advertiser's server, rather than the server of the Web page in which it is embedded, and so both servers effectively record the usage of the Web page. This technique is capable of capturing Web-wide information.

Limitations for Web-Wide Monitoring. Web bugs raise some serious privacy concerns, as they can effectively track an *individual user* across the Web (Bugnosis, 2000). Effectively, a profile of the user's browsing behavior is compiled, which is kept without their knowledge or permission. In addition, the information captured is not comprehensive enough to monitor Web-wide usage, as Web bugs can only record information on the Web pages that contain them, and cannot record usage of non-HTML resources.

Browser modification. A user's browser can be modified to report the user's navigation behavior directly to a server whenever the user navigates to a new page. Google adopts this approach with its GoogleBar technology (Google, 2002), but uses it to increase and continuously update its database of indexed Web pages and hyperlinks.

Limitations for Web-Wide Monitoring. Such an approach requires the user to explicitly install the browser update. Furthermore, this approach requires a large user base for it to work, and so can only be implemented by large companies such as search engines or portals, who, understandably, would be reluctant to provide open access to such information.

Migrating Web Resources

In previous papers (Evans and Furnell, 2001; Evans and Furnell, 2002), we have proposed that the Domain Name System (DNS) is becoming increasingly unsuitable for use as the Web's principle name resolution service. Specifically:

- The DNS is designed to map a hostname onto an IP address, whereas the Web needs a system to map a resource name onto a location
- The DNS deliberately constrains its namespace as it only has to deal with the names of servers, whereas the Web needs an unconstrained namespace to cater for all different types of resources and the needs of their owners
- Neither the DNS nor the Web's main resource identifier (the URL) has any way of storing and referencing a resource's time of creation
- Use of the DNS namespace by the URL prevents the resource from transparently migrating across servers

Our solution to these problems was the design of a new name resolution service called the Resource Locator Service (RLS), which was designed principally to:

- Provide an unconstrained namespace
- Enable resource migration
- Locate a resource according to its position in time as well as space

However, the RLS can also be used to monitor Web-wide resource usage, as it implicitly captures the usage of every *resource* requested by the clients that use it (see Evans and Furnell, 2001). In contrast, the

DNS is only queried for the IP address of every Web server. The RLS therefore provides an ideal platform for the design of a system to monitor Web-wide resource usage.

An Overview of the Resource Locator Service

The RLS has already been described in detail in Evans and Furnell (2001 and 2002). However, before discussing how it can be used to monitor Web resources, this section provides a brief overview of the service.

Architectural Overview

The RLS is designed to locate a resource when given its name, and can do so transparently to either the client, or the server. It is backward-compatible with all Web entities, ensuring it can be used wherever it is required. Its architecture comprises a distributed database, deployed across a network of nodes called Locators that form the RLS's Locator Network. A Locator performs a similar role to the DNS, but operates at the level of the individual resource, rather than at the level of the host (such as a Web server).

Figure 16.1 shows a high-level view of the RLS. The Locator Network provides the RLS's resolution service, mapping a resource's name onto its location, and redirecting the client to the resource's correct location using the HTTP redirect mechanism (Fielding et al., 1999). Although this is not the most efficient approach, it facilitates backward compatibility, enabling all Web entities to use the RLS.

In order for the client to find the Locator that holds the required name/location mapping, some form of mediation is required between the client and the Locator Network that can transparently route the client's request without requiring any modifications to the client or server. The RLS achieves this through the use of a Request Router, which routes HTTP requests to an appropriate Locator.

The Request Router

The Request Router (RR) is the key to the system. It is a scalable component that can route a request deterministically to any of more than 4 billion Locators, while adding only a single HTTP request and response as network overhead. In addition, it is extremely flexible,

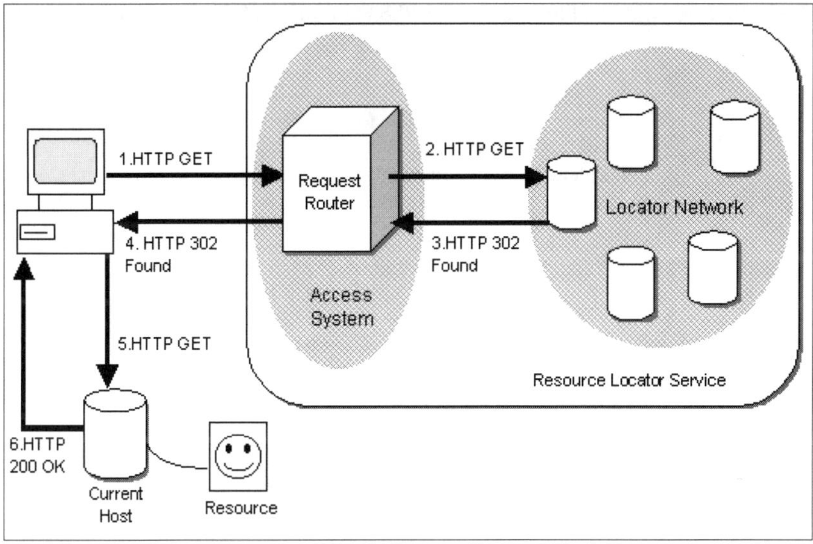

Figure 16.1 Architecture of the Resource Locator Service

and can be used wherever it is required, whether it be the client, server, or elsewhere in the network. It provides transparent, scalable mediation between the Web and the RLS through the use of a hash routing algorithm (based on the Cache Array Routing Protocol [CARP] [Valloppillil and Ross, 1998]), which takes a resource's name and maps it onto a hash space. The hash space is partitioned such that the name is mapped onto one and only one Locator (see Ross, 1997; Thaler and Ravishankar 1997). By requiring the Locators to be named according to a predetermined URL pattern that contains a zero-based linear numbering component (e.g., www.locator0.net, www.locator1.net, www.locator2.net), the name of the resource and the number of Locators in the system is all that is required to identify the appropriate Locator. In addition, the load across the nodes is equally balanced, yet there is no inter-node communication, virtually eliminating network overhead (see Evans and Furnell, 2001).

Scalability

A prototype of the RLS has been developed and presented in Evans and Furnell (2001). The prototype showed that the Request Router took only 0.718 seconds to find the appropriate Locator in a system of

Table 16.1 Overhead Introduced by the RLS with Different Configurations

Number of Locators	Download time for www.lycos.co.uk (time without RLS = 7.608 sec)	Overhead
1	8.477 seconds	**0.869 secs**
1,000	8.483 seconds	**0.875 secs**
10,000	8.546 seconds	**0.938 secs**
100,000	9.190 seconds	**1.582 secs**
1,000,000	15.985 seconds	**8.377 secs**

100,000 Locators, each of which can potentially hold the name/location information of millions of resources (see Table 16.1 and Figure 16.2). Total added latency was just 1.582 seconds, but a more optimal design should significantly reduce this figure.

Flexibility

The RR acts as an index into the distributed nodes of the Locator Network. Because it is decoupled from the RLS, it can be deployed virtually anywhere on the Web. For example, it can be:

- Embedded into an HTML document as a Java applet, ActiveX control, or even script
- Built into a browser
- Designed as a browser plug-in
- Built into a server, or added as a server module
- Embedded within a proxy server or a reverse proxy server

In this way, the RR can be integrated into the Web at whichever part of the Web's architecture it is required.

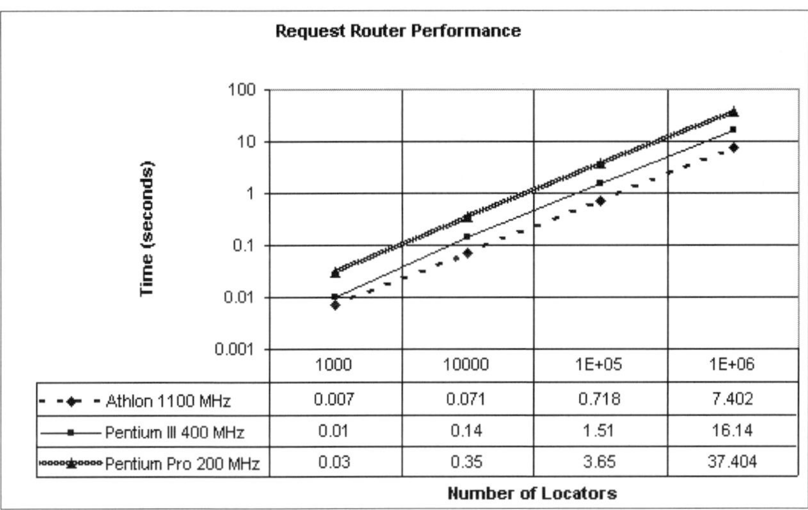

Figure 16.2 Performance of the Request Router

Extending the Resource Locator Service to Monitor Web Resource Usage

The RLS was primarily designed to enable resource migration on the Web. In this section, we present a model that shows how the RLS can be extended to capture Web-wide usage information by recording details of the location queries made to it. In order to maintain efficiency, the model is designed as a separate system, called the Web Resource Usage Monitor (WebRUM), which integrates with the RLS.

Architectural Overview of WebRUM

WebRUM comprises a distributed database whose nodes are accessed using a Request Router specific to the system (specifically, the URL pattern http://www.nodeX.WebRUM.net should be used). Each time a client queries the RLS, information about the query (such as the resource requested, a user-session identifier, etc.) is passed on to the appropriate WebRUM node using a WebRUM RR. In this way, WebRUM captures comprehensive usage information on resources from across the Web (see Figure 16.3).

Because it uses a Request Router, all information for a specific resource is contained on one WebRUM node, thus significantly

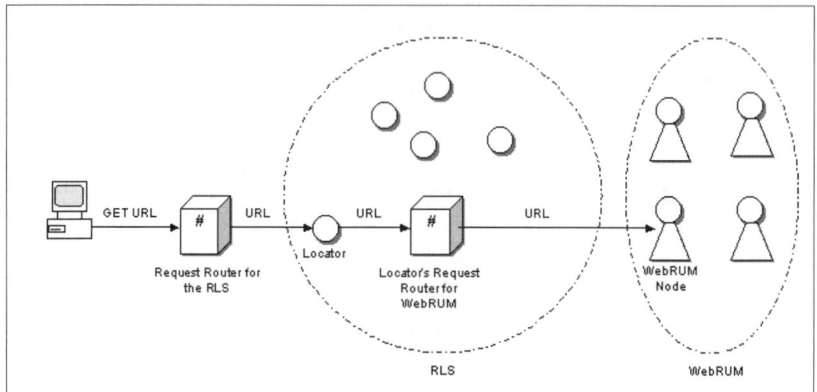

Figure 16.3 How WebRUM Integrates with the RLS

reducing the network overhead. Furthermore, WebRUM derives no information from the response of the server, as both it and the RLS are independent from the server's operation. As such, queries for resources that are not registered with the RLS are not passed on to WebRUM, thus preventing WebRUM from monitoring the usage of resources that cannot be located.

Addressing Privacy Concerns

WebRUM's ability to monitor usage of resources clearly has the potential to raise concerns in relation to privacy, both for the user and the resource owner.

User's Privacy

For WebRUM to be adopted, it must enable individual users to retain their anonymity, yet still enable individual user sessions to be recorded. The RLS enforces this by making the user's IP address or hostname persistent yet anonymous (e.g., by using a hash function), and passing this onto WebRUM. In this way, the same identifier used across different HTTP requests from the same user session can be persisted, but WebRUM cannot use it to identify the specific user. In cases where a single IP address represents a location with multiple users served by a domain name server; cookies could be used to identify individual users as long as users have the ability to opt out of the monitoring service. Any of these schemes would only identify the same user coming in over the same computer; they would not allow the same cataloging to be done if the user came in from another location altogether or a different computer on the same network.

Privacy of the Resource Owner

Not all resource owners will want their resources monitored. As such, the model requires a mechanism with which a resource owner can opt out of the monitoring service. Currently, we envisage using the Robots Exclusion Protocol (Koster, 1994) for this purpose, which was designed to restrict the access Web spiders (e.g., search engine indexing crawlers) are given to a Web server, and is now widely adopted. WebRUM can use the protocol to determine which resources can and cannot be monitored.

Defining the Information Stored by WebRUM

The information captured by WebRUM is a combination of that contained within existing Web server log files, and the client's HTTP request header. Tables 16.2 and 16.3 show the information stored by log files that are compliant with the two most common log file formats, the Common Log Format (CLF, defined in Luotonen, 1995) and the Extended Common Log Format (ECLF, defined in Hallam-Baker and Behlendorf, 1996). As can be seen, some of this information, such as Request Processing Time, is server-specific, and so of no use to WebRUM, while other items of information, such as Response Code, is returned by the server, and so is not accessible. As such, WebRUM must use what it can from these log files, plus some items of information extracted from the HTTP request. Table 16.4 shows the minimum set of information that WebRUM must store.

Accessing WebRUM's Information

To retrieve information about a specific resource, a client application needs the name of the resource (usually its URL), and a WebRUM RR. The resource name acts as an index into WebRUM, identifying the WebRUM node that stores the usage information for that resource. Once the appropriate node is found, retrieving the required information from it will depend upon the type of query the user wishes to make. To facilitate this, we intend to use the newly defined XQuery

Table 16.2 Fields Contained Within the Common Log Format (Luotonen, 1995)

Field	Description
Remote host	Remote hostname or IP address of client
Remote logname	The remote logname of the user (i.e., the logname the user uses to log onto their current client. In practice, this information is rarely present).
Authenticated username	User's username (note that this will only be present if the associated resource requires that the user authenticate herself before the resource can be transferred).
Date	Date and time of the request
Request line	The request line of the request header (i.e., Method, URL, and protocol version)
Response code	The HTTP status code returned to the client
Bytes	The content length of the resource returned to the client

Table 16.3 Additional Commonly Supported Fields Used in ECLF Log Files (Krishnamurthy and Rexford, 2001)

Field	Description
Referer	The URL of the Web page from where the resource was requested
Request Processing Time	The length of time taken from when the request was received to when the response was sent
User Agent	The name and other details of the application that sent the request. Information can include such details as operating system and hardware platform upon which the application was running.

Table 16.4 Information Stored by WebRUM

Field	Description
Remote host	Anonymized hostname of client
Referer	The URL of the Web page from where the resource was requested.
User Agent	The name and other details of the application that sent the request. Information can include such details as operating system and hardware platform upon which the application was running.
Date	Date and time of the request (recorded by the WebRUM node at the time it receives the information from the Locator (GMT), formatted according to RFC 1123 (Braden, 1989).
Request line	The request line of the request header (i.e., Method, URL, and protocol version)
Language	The language that the client requires the resource to be in, as specified by the Accept-Language header of the initial request

query language (Boag et al., 2002), enabling the user to send an SQL-like query formatted in XML to the appropriate WebRUM node via HTTP. At present, however, this feature is undefined.

Applications of WebRUM

Some examples of the types of queries that could be answered by WebRUM include:

- What are the most/least popular resources/images/Web pages etc. on the Web?
- How have the most/least popular resources changed over time?
- How have the most/least popular resources changed during significant events (e.g., The Queen's Golden Jubilee, September 11th)?
- Which languages are the most popular on the Web?
- Which countries use the Web the most/least?
- How many bytes of information are transferred in a given period of time?

- How many resources/images/Web pages/etc. are there on the Web?

Such statistics provide insight into the changing nature of the online society, and of society in general. However, WebRUM can also act as a platform for the provision of other services that cannot currently be provided, as the following sub-sections describe.

Enhanced Navigation

WebRUM can enhance the user's ability to navigate the Web by dynamically providing information about a hyperlink *before* the user clicks on it. In this way, the user can make a more informed judgment on whether to see the resource referenced by the hyperlink before "rewarding" it with a hit.

Figure 16.4 shows how this can be achieved. A proxy server intercepts the client's request for a Web page, and queries WebRUM to determine the number of times the hyperlinks within the Web page have been clicked. The proxy then dynamically inserts the usage information into the Web page, enabling the user to see at a glance the popularity of each hyperlink. This is a trivial example of how WebRUM's information can be used to enhance user navigation. Other studies have found strong regularities in users' browsing behavior (e.g., Hochheiser and Schneiderman, 1999; Huberman et al., 1998), indicating that more complex heuristics can be applied to WebRUM's information to further enhance navigation.

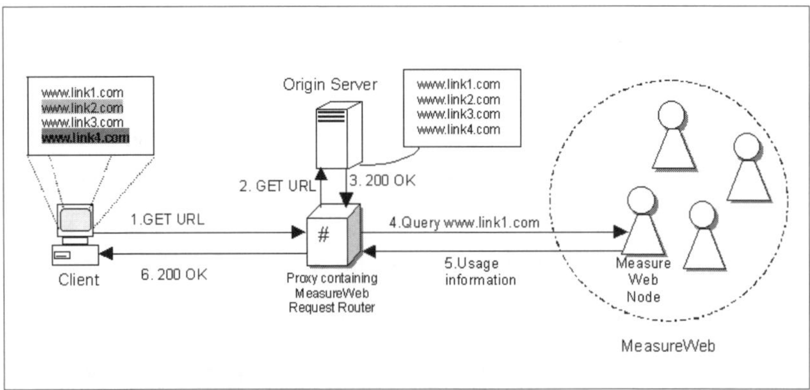

Figure 16.4 Using WebRUM to Enhance Navigation

Charting the Web's Traffic Patterns

Many experiments have been conducted that attempt to display the structure of the Web (see Dodge and Kitchin, 2001, for examples). However, each researcher has had to spend valuable time and resources gaining the necessary data from a (usually small) sample of users in order to run their experiment. WebRUM can greatly aid such experiments by providing instantly available data that can be mined with the appropriate tools.

In addition, WebRUM will be able to provide far more detail, providing dynamic charts that provide the Web site owner with information such as:

- Which hyperlinks linking to the owner's resource provide the most/least traffic?
- How many people visit the Web pages that link to the owner's resource?
- How much traffic does a Web page direct to the owner's resource compared with the traffic that the page directs to other resources?
- Which hyperlinks on the Web would provide the most/least traffic?

Issues and Further Work

WebRUM could change the nature of the Web fundamentally, providing a unique tool for exploring the changing interests of society. However, there are a number of issues that must be addressed if it is to be deployed successfully:

- WebRUM relies upon wide adoption of the RLS: The RLS is still in prototype form, and so WebRUM cannot be developed in the near future. However, the two systems can be separated, enabling WebRUM to be self-supporting if necessary.
- Performance: WebRUM can scale to support over 4 billion individual nodes. However, the processing and network demands on each node may be huge, depending upon the nature and volume of queries sent to it. In addition,

collating information from across WebRUM nodes would increase the load and network overheads of the system. Further work must examine the use of caching techniques and distinct caching servers that simply return results to common queries in order to manage the load.

- Security: WebRUM nodes may be at risk from Denial of Service attacks (Krishnamurthy and Rexford, 2001). In addition, care should be taken to ensure only genuine RLS Locators provide the usage information.

We are examining the potential for developing the RLS and WebRUM as an OPES (Open Pluggable Edge Servers) content service. OPES is an emerging specification for the design of intelligent edge servers that sit in the content path (i.e., the path of entities between the client and server) (Tomlinson, 2001). These servers will form a new layer of content services that operate above the Web. Further work will see a client's request being intercepted by an Edge Server, routed to the appropriate RLS Locator, and recorded via WebRUM. OPES therefore provides a promising platform for the provision of our services.

Conclusion

We have presented a model for monitoring Web-wide resource usage that has the potential to reveal insights into society, including its hopes, fears, interests and concerns. In addition, the model can provide a powerful tool for Web site owners and advertisers, providing an independent source of quality marketing information. Although there is much work still to be done, we believe the concept of measuring Web-wide resource usage has the potential to transform the Web.

References

Boag, S., Chamberlin, D., and Fernandez, M., Florescu, D., Robie, J., Simeon, J., and Stefanescu, M. (2002). "XQuery 1.0: An XML Query Language," *W3C Working Draft*, 30th April 2002. Available: http://www.w3.org/TR/xquery

Braden, R. (1989). "Requirements for Internet Hosts - Communication layers, STD 3," *RFC 1123*, October 1989.

Bugnosis (2000). "Web Bug FAQ," Available: http://www.bugnosis.org/faq.html

Dodge, M., and Kitchin, R., (2001). *Atlas of cyberspace.* Addison Wesley, London.

Evans, M. P., and Furnell, S. M. (2001). "The Resource Locator Service: Fixing a Flaw in the Web", *Computer Networks*, Vol. No 37 (3–4) (2001): 307–330, November 2001.

Evans, M. P., and Furnell, S. M. (2002). "A Web-Based Resource Migration Protocol Using WebDAV," in: *Proceedings of the Eleventh International World Wide Web Conference*, Honolulu, Hawaii, May 7th-11th 2002. Available: http://www2002.org/CDROM/refereed/359/index.html

Fielding, R, Gettys, J., Mogul, J. C., Nielsen, H. F., Masinter, L., Leach, P., and Berners-Lee, T. (1999). "HyperText Transfer Protocol – HTTP/1.1," *RFC 2616*, June 1999. Available: http://www.ietf.org/rfc/rfc2616.txt

Google (2002). Google Toolbar page. Available: http://toolbar.google.com/

Google (2004). Google Search Engine Web site. Available: http://www.google.com

Hallam-Baker, P. M., and Behlendorf, B. (1996). Extended Log File Format. Available: http://www.w3.org/TR/WD-logfile.html, March 1996

Hochheiser, H., and Schneiderman, B. (1999). "Understanding Patterns of User Visits to Web Sites: Interactive Starfield Visualizations of WWW Log Data," In: *Proceedings of ASIS '99*, 1999.

Huberman, B. A., Pirolli, P. L. T., Pitkow, J. E., and Lukse, R. M. (1998). "Strong Regularities in World Wide Surfing," *Science*, Vol. 280, 3rd April 1998.

Koster, M., (1994). "A Standard for Robot Exclusion." Available: http://www.robotstxt.org/wc/norobots.html

Krishnamurthy, B., and Rexford, J. (2001). *Web protocols and practice: HTTP 1.1, networking protocols, caching, and traffic measurement.* Addison Wesley, 2001.

Luotonen, A. (1995). "The Common Logfile Format," July 1995. Available: http://www.w3.org/Daemon/User/Config/Logging.html.

Ross, K. W. (1997). "Hash Routing for Collections of Shared Web Caches," *IEEE Network*, November/December 1997: 37–44.

Thaler, D. G., and Ravishankar, C. V. (1998). "Using Name Based Mappings to Increase Hit Rates," *IEEE/ACM Transactions on Networking*, 6(1), Feb. 1998.

Tomlinson, G., Chen, R., and Hofmann, M. (2001). "A Model for Open Pluggable Edge Services," Internet Draft draft-tomlinson-opes-model-00.txt

Valloppillil, V., and Ross, K. W. (1998). "Cache Array Routing Protocol v1.0," Internet Draft, draft-vinod-carp-v1-02.txt, February 26, 1998. Available: http://www.cs-ipv6.lancs.ac.uk/ipv6/documents/standards/general-comms/internet-drafts/draft-vinod-carp-v1-03.txt

CHAPTER 17

A Vision of the Internet in 2010

Paul Reynolds
Orange PCS and University of Plymouth

Background

In this chapter I articulate a vision of the Internet in 2010, in other words, just a few years from now. The vision is one that fully supports all forms of mobility including personal, terminal, session, and code. It is, in effect, a Mobile Internet.

The 2010 Internet will be characterized by a move away from intelligence within the network (3rd Generation mobile network architecture) or at the edges (current Internet architecture) to intelligence everywhere. The 2010 Internet will have an all Internet Engineering Task Force (IETF) protocol-based access, core, and service networks with effective quality management. It will be underpinned by Mobile-IPv6, which is adaptable to mobile networks, having adequate addressing capacity, multicast management, security mechanisms, and mobility management.

2010 Internet Requirements

The 2010 Internet will be required to support:

- Terminal, personal, session, and code mobility
- Roaming and fast-hand-off between different access networks
- Quality comparable with telecommunications networks
- Global and seamless service provision
- Data rates starting at 2Mbit/s and ranging up to 1Gbit/s

- Highly distributed terminals
- Managed Quality of Service (QoS)
- Any air interface specification that may be required to achieve higher bit rates and improve spectrum utilization
- Capacity for several radio interfaces depending on the context
- "Smart antenna" processing

Extrapolating Technology Trends to a Vision

One method to provide a vision for the 2010 Internet is to extrapolate from current technology trends, the most significant for the next eight years being:

- More technology in the user space, not less
- Increased user literacy
- More open, and less standardized, interfaces
- Greater impact of nomadic computing as terminal devices become more portable; Internet and telecommunications convergence supporting QoS management
- Software dominance over hardware
- Greater transparency to technology complexity
- Automated and autonomously initiated machine-to-machine interactions
- Much reduced time to market
- Shorter service life cycles
- Smaller and faster micro-chips
- Smaller and smarter user terminals
- Commodity networks

These trends are supported by a number of enabling technologies including:

- Low-cost embedded, even disposable, radio microchips and software-defined radio systems supporting dynamic configuration of the air interface and dynamic spectrum allocation, i.e., possibly no operator ownership of unique spectrum
- Mobile software agents, supporting personal profiles and personalization of data, and intelligent agents learning, adapting, and acting on behalf of a user even pre-empting their needs and wishes. These agents will require minimal user involvement, i.e., the technology complexity is hidden from the user
- Pervasive network of sensors, ad-hoc networking, distributed mobility management, middleware to support homogeny, autonomous adaptive networks that self-manage their structure to meet ever-changing demands
- Software-defined network elements

Drivers to Achieve the Vision

The vision for the 2010 Internet will not be incarnated without a sense of purpose or drive from the user community. These users will demand:

- Applications that require “extreme bit rates” such as the 1Gbit/s
- Applications that are “mobile aware”
- Not just “IP technology,” also “IP thinking”
- User-centric, bespoke services
- Ubiquitous computing and context awareness
- Distributed mobility management including inter- and intratechnology hand-off
- Ad-hoc networking
- Open architectures for reconfigurabilty of all layers of the management

- Enhanced privacy and security
- Soft networking
- Scalable middleware deployments
- Flexible and reconfigurable radio architectures
- Radically improved battery technology

The drive for the distribution of intelligence will result in:

- Intelligence on the move (mobile agents)
- Virtual-home environments
- Service provisioning based on software downloading
- Cognitive radio systems

2010 Internet Vision

Based upon these requirements, trends, and drivers it is possible to envisage the Internet in the year 2010. It can be perceived as comprising three parts: an access, a core, and a service network.

2010 Internet Access Network

The 2010 Internet access network will be characterized by an improved capacity from the available spectrum and a move away from a cellular-only system to one that integrates broadcast, cellular, cordless, Wireless LAN, point-to-multipoint, and fixed access technologies. There will be a need to support more elaborate radio access technologies and allow, for example, adaptive signal processing at both the base station and terminal. The access network will:

- Have a mixed-mode radio interface with rapid adaptation to bursty traffic; for example, to support a digital terrestrial television return channel and its adaptation to asymmetrical bit rates
- Use smart antennas at both the base station and terminal. The radio interface will be designed to take advantage of them; for example, to include signaling to allow enhanced antenna processing

- Support dynamic allocation of spectrum as loading demands
- Use of spread spectrum techniques
- Use Internet Engineering Task Force (IETF) protocols for mobility and hand-off management with consequence of openness toward radio networks, with a generic "IP over wireless" interface, that can be adapted to several radio interfaces

There will be a need to relieve the expensive 3rd Generation Mobile Network spectrum whenever possible, and to offer higher bit rates to nomadic customers when they are in a static situation by way of unregulated spectrum, for example, wireless local area networks (LAN).

The 2010 Internet will integrate broadcasting services, notably “IP push” services. Different degrees of integration will be possible with an “intelligent” server hiding complexity to the user and server. This approach raises considerable technical and regulatory challenges because it implies cooperation of heterogeneous networks that may be operated by different enterprise entities.

The use of broadband coverage of specific areas or “hot spots”; for example, hotels, congress centers, and airports will be provided albeit at the cost of a restricted mobility data access with techniques derived from wireless local area networks.

Complementary fixed access networks such as Asymmetrical Distal Subscribe Line (ADSL) and the domestic cordless networks can be expected to be found in most households by 2010. For example, a Bluetooth access point connected to an ADSL modem will allow mobile terminals to connect to a mobile network without loading the air interface of the mobile network; i.e., ADSL provides a tunnel to the mobile network. The mobile terminal will have become a universal terminal, for example, supporting telephony and remote controls.

2010 Internet “Core Network”

The 2010 Internet will comprise a single universal network that will be capable of supporting all types of access, fixed and mobile. Mobile operators will find that their core networks will evolve toward more open and universal solutions capable of supporting fixed, mobile, and broadcasting, allowing them to interwork more deeply than they do today.

Intelligent mobile agents will exist throughout the network and in user devices and will act continually to simplify tasks and ensure transparency.

2010 Internet "Service Network"

For the user, Service Network will be capable of supporting:

- Access to services via the best access route, in terms of cost and bit rate, without the need to manage several environments
- Access to much higher bit rates in "static" situations and when the required information is not personalized, i.e., broadcast
- "Capacity-aware" accesses that adapt to and make use of the available bit rate, for example, to synchronize files in relation to a distant computer, to download attached files, etc., when the availability of a broadband network has been detected
- Access to the same services via variable data rates by way of content adaptation or application transcoding. This will entail the adaptation of service presentation before being transmitted so that its size can be adapted to the bit rate available. This implies variable rate coding for voice and video, but also variable contents format or even service adaptation, for example, deleting or reducing images, deleting access to certain applications

Discussion

The 2010 Internet can be defined as a simplified access for the user to all of their services across multiple radio technologies and networks. Their services adapting, notably to the available bit rate, without forcing them to manage the consequential complexities.

The 2010 Internet will be delivered over time. Starting with the introduction of nomadic services, for example, broadband access in "hot spots" via a wireless local area network (WLAN) connected to a fixed network; access to the mobile network via a home radio interface and a "tunnel" through the fixed network. Later, it will evolve toward a more generic solution making the support for services by different networks easier, including:

- The implementation of QoS management protocols and parameters recognizable by all types of networks; each network being able to map the QoS protocols and parameters to its own requirements, for example, radio resource allocation
- Generalization of IPv6 and the emergence of consistent solutions for IPv4/IPv6 interworking
- Convergence of security policies, for example, based on an Authentication, Authorization, and Accounting (AAA) architecture on the network side and the SIM card on the terminal side

It will be possible to use differing technologies to support services in a way to optimize performance and cost trade-offs. These technologies include:

- Auto-adaptation of services to the available bit rate and to the terminal capabilities
- Flexible access networks capable of easily integrating new radio interfaces, allowing the implementation of higher performance radio solutions; for example, increased user peak bit rate, increased physical layer spectral efficiency, more efficient resource allocation
- Continuous connection to the mobile network via radio access technologies optimized for different contexts; for example, indoor-outdoor new frequency bands
- Applications taking advantage of the changes in communication conditions—for example, to automatically carry out certain heavy tasks when the available bit rate is increased
- Universal core network, evolution of fixed IP networks
- Multi-interface terminals, programmable at the radio level

Along with this evolution, the 2010 Internet will need to deal with:

- The degree to which operators can control services and service access when terminals are becoming more powerful
- Different business models between mobile operators, ISPs, and WLAN “hot spot” operators
- Regulatory hurdles, including limitations and ambiguities on the use of wireless LAN frequencies for access to a public network, and using broadcasting frequencies for combining telecommunications and broadcasting services

Conclusion

The 2010 Internet will be able to support mobility. The division of mobile telecommunication networks and the Internet will be bridged and a single unifying technology IETF protocols will support mobility and ubiquitous computing.

CHAPTER 18

The One-Room Schoolhouse (Internet Portal) for K-12 Schools

John W. Collins, Jr.
Assistant Professor, Education Leadership, Management and Policy, Seton Hall University

In addition to the current *No Child Left Behind* (NCLB) legislation, for the past few years there has been a renewed national resurgence toward K-12 standards and accountability. This has direct implications for education at all levels. What? Why? How? Any major momentum shakes the very core of our profession. Many educators contend we must have a knowledge base, standards, and appropriate preparation programs. Most readers would agree the accountability issue is connected to the standards. In other words, to what standards are we accountable? This chapter starts the dialogue with education leadership standards. Standards for students and teachers are obvious continuations from that backdrop and can be included under the appropriate themes that will emerge.

A Needs Assessment

Charles Achilles (et al., 2001) is a long-time advocate of building a K-12 knowledge base, standards, and appropriate education leader preparation programs. He is not alone; other advocates include Bok (1987), Boyan (1981), Haller and McNamara (1997), Hallinger and Heck (1996), Iannaccone (1976), McCarthy and Kuh (1988, 1998), Mitchel (2001), Murphy (1999), Ogawa (1994), Price (2000), Shepard and Smith (1990), Shipman (1996), and Van Meter (1997), to name just a few. The knowledge base dialogue is at least three decades old (Innacone, 1976). Achilles' most recent efforts with William Price

(2000, 2001) include the metaphor of using military officers (e.g., General Quickdraw) to run school districts. I find the allegory particularly poignant and will uncover the significance later in this article. Achilles and Price point out that military officers are educated and trained to have at their disposal all the possible knowledge and information available to make the most appropriate decision(s) for a given situation. Sometimes decisions have to be made with less than all the information, especially in time-sensitive situations. Hersey and Blanchard (1982) acknowledge these activities as situational leadership. Does this sound familiar in today's K-12 school environments? The author continually observes the need for a knowledge base in multiple K-12 settings during his in-service work, consulting, mentoring, teaching, and professional conferences. Achilles refers to this as what is missing in the current debate about education standards: a knowledge base. Without the appropriate knowledge base, how can we deal with standards, accountability, preparation programs, in-service development, student achievement, etc.? Suffice it to say there are large numbers of practitioners and academics that support the concept of a K-12 knowledge base. The real challenge is to pull together the research, theory, consensually validated exemplary professional practice (informed professional judgment) into one place that can be easily and quickly accessed. This author is convinced that the reason a knowledge base has not been developed in the past 30 years is that it is considered too hard to assimilate.

The Magnitude

Today's K-12 educators have to master a multitude of concepts, skills, and competencies. Consider this partial list for instance: accountability, assessment, building and facility maintenance, collective bargaining, class size, constructivism, curriculum monitoring, equipment maintenance, ethics, evaluations, financing, gifted and talented programs, grants and corporate partnerships, instructional delivery, leasing, legal requirements, new building construction, observations, outsourcing, problem-based learning, personnel management, planning, reorganization, research and statistical inferences, right-sizing, school board savvy, school choice, school violence, special education, staff development, state and local standards, teacher-pupil ratios, technology integration, transformational leadership, transportation, unionization, and multitudes of forever-evolving reform initiatives. Although many of these topics have been associated exclusively with school administrations for decades, other K-12 educators are becoming involved and nearly all of these subjects have succumbed to change. Change is certainly the expectation of most school districts—to the point it has become the only thing school administrators can absolutely anticipate. For a visual aid, review the list in Figure 18.1. The circle of arrows depicts the constant change. On top of this list, consider the various homogeneous and heterogeneous environments: urban, suburban, rural, multicultural, multilingual, public, private, charter, magnet, affluent, poor, middle-class, political polarization, vocational, alternative, continuing education, continental U.S., the states and territories, overseas ... and add any of your own personal experiences. Tie this all together within the economic, political, and social makeup of any particular school district setting and we can start to understand the complexity of K-12 education in the 21st century.

Most of us are not capable of working 24/7 (at least not for very long), to do everything that needs to be done. Expectations are becoming that our K-12 educators need to be superhuman or supereducators. The structure in our school districts is very finite and already overburdened with myriad responsibilities. The only way we can expect educators to be successful is through the help of everyone involved in our school systems. Some of the supporting constituents can include: the school board, parents, teachers, community leaders, students, staff, administrator preparation programs, higher education partnerships, cross-district partnerships, etc. Thomas Sergiovanni (1996, 2000) refers to such activities as establishing learning communities. Roland Barth (1990, 2000) advocates such solutions that come from within our school districts. Bill Gates (1996, 1999) adds the technology component and calls them Connected Learning Communities. All of these ideals of community conglomerates are truly appealing provided they can be balanced to assist with engaged learning. This is where education leadership and vision have to be deftly applied, so that no single constituent is favored over any other—a critical juggling act to say the least.

accountability	outsourcing
assessment	problem-based learning
building and facility maintenance	personnel management
collective bargaining	planning
class size	pupil – teacher ratios
constructivism	reorganization
curriculum monitoring	research and statistical inferences
equipment maintenance	right-sizing
ethics	school board savvy
evaluations	school choice
financing	school violence
gifted and talented programs	special education
grants and corporate partnerships	staff development
instructional delivery	state and local standards
leasing	technology integration
legal requirements	transformational leadership
new building construction	transportation
observations	unionization

Figure 18.1 Partial List of K-12 Education Concepts, Skills, and Competencies for Standards

The Silver Bullet

So why are some people convinced that a single concept can pull everything together like a magical silver bullet? The author is convinced that the typical critic has not been fully informed or educated. Even multiple silver bullets cannot fully encompass the majority of most school settings. Many nonprofit organizations are constantly working to improve the knowledge base and access to the issues. A few examples include NEA, AFT, AASA, NSBA, Elementary/Secondary Principal Associations, and the regional education laboratories.

This chapter is designed to be primer for evaluating, analyzing, and synthesizing all of the resources that are currently available, using educational technology, specifically the Internet, to create a

K-12 knowledge base. Not wanting to be categorized as a techno zealot, the author leans on the theses of Robert Evans (1996) and Neil Postman (1993). Evans believes that *caring* is critical to the change process from within schools. Evans's thesis is that any new idea, reform, or school change is done by leaders who recognize their colleagues' strengths and build upon those strengths to the change implemented. Caring is italicized to represent the importance of this ideal and bring attention to those leaders who are not quite embracing the idea. Postman advocates our careful and deliberate thinking with the use of technology, even to the point that our societal fabric has become unraveled due to such failures.

The One-Room Schoolhouse Revisited

Consider the possibility of pulling everything together into a single room or space: a one-room schoolhouse for educators. Granted, the size of the information and data makes this a rather large space—more like a warehouse, but still accessible from a single and unbiased location. The Library of Congress (LOC) is a great example for books, periodicals, etc. We need our own LOC for K-12 schools. This is especially critical in view of governmental reorganization efforts that include the elimination of ERIC clearinghouses (Quint, April 2003). The current term is a *portal* to multiple data sources and information that can be accessed using the Internet. This concept works by having a central gateway to the information: research, theory, informed practice, and any list can be built upon. It is actually three-dimensional, with connections to height, width, and depth of a particular K-12 school topic.

The entire idea sounds like another ivory-tower approach that an academic dreamed up during a professional conference. With the foregoing backdrop, how is this approach different? First, the responsibilities of educators are real—not ivory-tower metaphors. Information needs to be readily available and accurate to deal with daily and often critical school district issues. There must be an ability to tailor the information request to the various environments. For instance, what may work in a rural school district is not necessarily generalizable to an urban district and vice versa. Second, if we carefully select reliable information sources and group by themes we accomplish dichotomous caring: one axis that provides information in different K-12 environments and another axis that ensures we consider the various social, economic, and political viewpoints (see Figure 18.2). Try to imagine the LOC and a warehouse. Both are huge entities. Without thoughtful organization, quickly finding a specific item is next to impossible. The proverb "like trying to finding a needle in a haystack" seems to be a perfect fit for our situation.

Feasibility and Challenges

After additional review many readers may still be skeptical. This is too much pie-in-the-sky for many. Postman would remind us to clearly think through any potential uses of technology with the human dimension clearly considered. So it is imperative that K-12 educators can communicate and network with each other. Great, yet another requirement added to the one-room schoolhouse for K-12 schools. How is this all possible? The author recommends using a portal model that already works. The military has at least one and Achilles would be proud. It belongs to the U.S. Army under the name of (surprise) the Army Knowledge Online (AKO). The author has access to this portal due to his retirement from that service after nearly 23 years of active duty. The portal can be personally adjusted with a specialized profile. In other words the opening screens can be modified to deal with all the issues addressed in this chapter. There is also the capability to network and e-mail colleagues from within the portal. Sections of the user profile could cover private, public, rural,

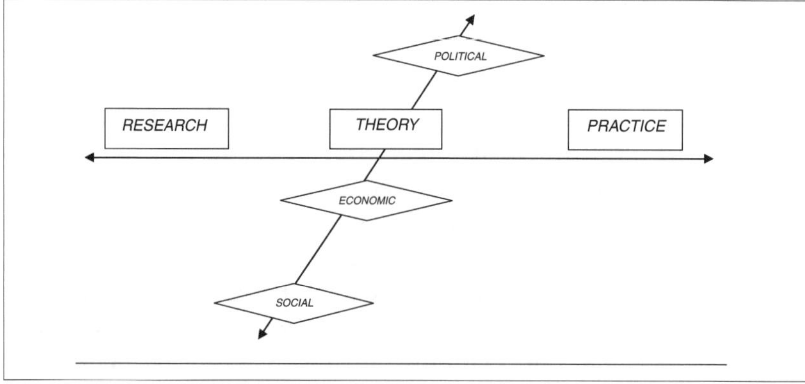

Figure 18.2 Axes of K-12 School Knowledge Base

urban, suburban, political, economic, social resources, etc. under the headings of research, theory, and sound practice. Just to reinforce Barth's assertion that K-12 solutions must come from within the schools, the existing Army portal did not have any K-12 research, theory, or sound practice attributed to General Quickdraw. (Chuck Achilles—it is okay to smile now.) As a conceptual framework, view Figure 18.3. This framework is just a starting point, not some all-inclusive model carved into stone. Additions and modifications are expected and needed for all learning communities. The dialogue needs your input.

No matter how careful a particular organization is at assembling information, the preponderance is constituent-based. More succinctly stated, organizations are products of our social, economic, and political systems. The author proposes the establishment of a K-12 education portal that puts many silver bullets into a single warehouse—a warehouse full of silver bullets or at least entry points to the required information. Further, this effort should be sponsored by a nonprofit foundation that is motivated solely by the prospect of improving K-12 schools, administration, and overall student achievement. No one individual or groups of individuals can build this portal. It will take the collaborative efforts of many K-12 constituencies. The point here is that all K-12 knowledge and information needs to be available through one portal. There should be no commercials, advertisement, or marketing: truly nonprofit (as opposed to not-for-profit). Additionally, there are many connections in this portal for supporting all members of a given learning community, e.g., parents, students, school boards, and local business partners.

Conclusion

This chapter briefly covers the need, feasibility, and a potential solution to the three-decade dialogue for a K-12 school knowledge base. The major components are recommended to cover research, theory and sound practice within a multitude of environments: public, private, urban, suburban, and rural. The connection to social, economic, and political implications for each is equally critical. The author proposes the establishment of a One-Room Schoolhouse (Portal) for K-12 Schools under the auspices of a nonprofit organization. One existing knowledge base portal was discussed to help skeptics see that this

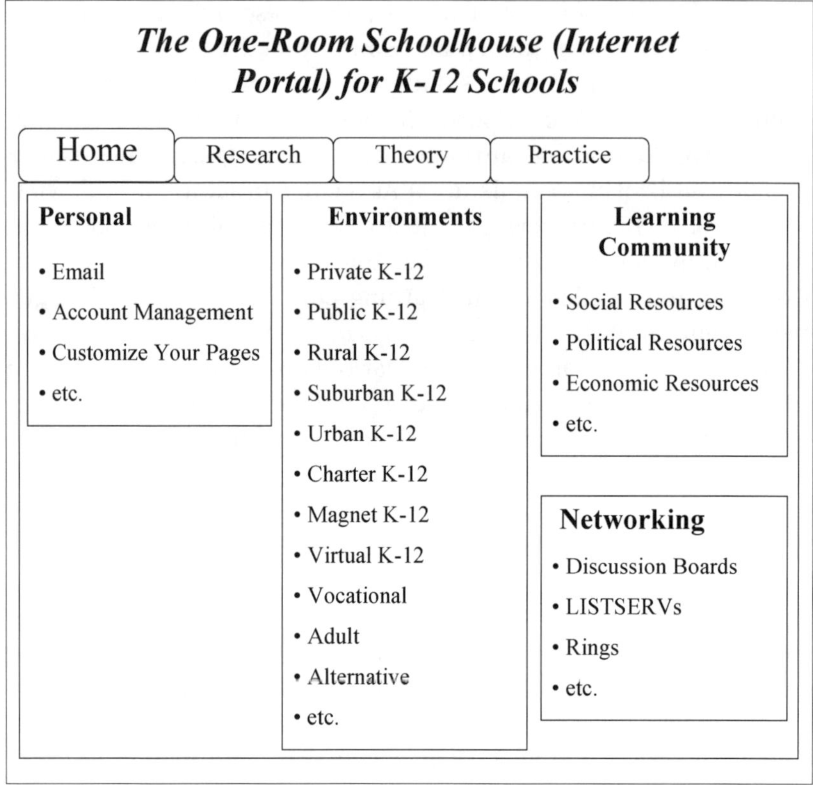

Figure 18.3 A Conceptual Framework—Potential Categories, Topics, Hyperlinks, Resources, etc. (What, Why, and How of K-12 schools)

endeavor is very feasible. Additionally there are many connections for all members of a given learning community as well. This author is convinced that if the portal is built, many will come … so that our voices from within the schools can be heard and more importantly shared.

About the University

Seton Hall University, founded in 1856, is the nation's largest and oldest diocesan Catholic university. Seton Hall welcomes and educates men and women of all races, creeds, and ethnic origins. The

University is distinguished by its commitment to liberal arts and professional education.

Located on 58 acres in the suburban Village of South Orange, New Jersey (just 14 miles from New York City), Seton Hall is home to nine schools and colleges including the College of Education and Human Services. Through its schools and colleges, the university offers more than 40 undergraduate majors and programs and 45 graduate programs. Seton Hall offers outstanding facilities to assist students in meeting their educational goals. An example of this commitment to ultramodern facilities is the recently opened Walsh Library, which offers the resources and technology required for the highest quality academic study and research.

EDUCAUSE Awards for Excellence in Campus Networking

1999 Winner: Seton Hall University

Seton Hall sees information technology as a means for achieving its institutional mission: to prepare future leaders in a global society. In 1995, the first of two five-year technology plans was enacted. This 5,500-student institution made a $15-million investment in new network infrastructure and services to improve teaching, learning, and administration. One of the most visible aspects of the plan is the Mobile Computing Program under which all first-year students are issued a laptop computer (refreshed every two years) as part of their tuition and fees. All residence halls provide data connections for each student; one-third of the classrooms have data and power connections to each seat and built-in computer projection equipment.

The Division of Technology has doubled its professional staffing since 1995, and its faculty and curriculum development budget of $250,000 per year supports projects in seven departments. The underlying approach has been to adopt a common interface to online course material to simplify student navigation of the campus curriculum. The SHU Institute for Technology Assessment and Support, which provides a clearinghouse for best practices in planning, support, and assessment of IT in education, has received significant outside support. Administratively, a major reengineering project targeted Enrollment Services, which now offers many services on the Web. Special initiatives include SHU's partnership in the Essex

County Training Center, providing technology training to elementary and secondary school teachers in a statewide effort to improve teaching. SHU also serves as one of two host sites for the Virtual Academic Library Environment (VALE), bringing online library resources to a consortium of 39 colleges and universities in New Jersey.

The technology vision of SHU is to establish a student-centered, network-centered, distributed learning environment whose core is a set of quality information services, especially academic services. This vision is being carried out through intelligent, focused, and creative planning as well as exemplary use of partnerships with commercial and other academic entities.

EDUCAUSE Award for Systemic Progress in Teaching and Learning

2000 Honorable Mention: Seton Hall University

Seton Hall has made a major commitment to information technology since 1995, with a plan focused on using technology in support of teaching and learning for its 5,500 students. The university developed its innovative Mobile Computing Program to make technology ubiquitous throughout the educational experience. Each student in the program—which is mandatory for all full-time entering undergraduates beginning with the class of 2002—is provided with a notebook computer as part of their tuition and fees; faculty are encouraged to integrate technology tools into the curriculum, with special "mobile" sections created for undergraduate core courses. Support services include the university's Teaching, Learning, and Technology Center, a Curriculum Development Initiative, and a Faculty Technology Fellows Program. An Institute for Technology Development is engaged in a longitudinal study on the impact of technology on the learning environment at Seton Hall and other institutions across the country, to serve as a national clearinghouse for best practices in the use of technology in teaching and learning as well as assessment data on the subject. A promotion and tenure policy specifically covers recognition of using technology in teaching, with a section on the scholarship of technology.

References

Achilles, C. M., and Price, W. J. (2001). "What is missing in the Current Debate about Education Administration (EDAD) Standards!" *The AASA Professor*, 24(2): 8–14.

Achilles, C. M. (1999). *Training programs in EDAD: Are they worth a Tinker's dam?* Paper at NCPEA. Jackson Hole, Wyoming.

Achilles, C. M. (1998). "How long?" *The AASA Professor*, 22(1): 9-12.

Achilles, C. M. (1987a). *The key triad: Why? What and How?* (ERIC Document 302 957 Available from http://www.edrs.com.)

Achilles, C. M. (1987b). *Toward a model for preparation programs for education's leaders.* (ERIC Document 302 959 Available from http://www.edrs.com.)

Barth, R. (1990). *Improving schools from within.* San Francisco, CA: Jossey-Bass, Inc.

Barth, R. (2000). *Preparing leaders for the 21st century.* San Francisco, CA: Jossey-Bass, Inc.

Bok, D. (1987). "The challenge to schools of education." *Harvard Magazine*, 89(5):47–57.

Boyan, N.J. (1981). "Follow the leader: Commentary on research in educational administration." *Educational Researcher*, 10(2): 6-13, 21.

Evans, R. (1996). *The human side of school change: Reform, resistance, and the real-life problems of innovation.* San Francisco, CA: Jossey-Bass, Inc.

Gates, B. (2000). *Business at the speed of thought: Succeeding in the digital economy.* New York: Warner Books.

Gates, B. (1996). *The road ahead.* New York: Penguin Books.

Hersey, P. and Blanchard, K. (1982). *Management of organizational behavior utilizing human resources.* Englewood Cliffs, N.J.: Prentice-Hall.

Haller, E. J., Brent, B. O. and McNamara, J. H. (1997). "Does graduate training in educational administration programs improve America's schools?" *Phi Delta Kappan*, 79(3), 222–227.

Hallinger, P., and Heck, R.H. (1996). "Reassessing the principal's role in school effectiveness: A review of empirical research, 1980-1995." *Educational Administration Quarterly*, 32(1): 5–44.

Innaccone, L. (1976). *50 Years of deed, program, and research in educational administration.* Tel Aviv: University of Tel Aviv. Conference Paper.

McCarthy, M. M., and Kuh, G. D. (1997). *Continuity and change: The educational leadership professorate.* Columbia, MO: UCEA.

McCarthy, M. M., Kuh, G. D., Newell, L. J., and Iacona, C. M. (1988). *Under scrutiny: The educational leadership professorate.* Tempe, AZ: UCEA.

Mitchel, C. P. (2001). "The quest for better preparation programs." *The AASA Professor,* 24(4):10–14.

Murphy, J. (1999). *The quest for a center: Notes on the state of the profession of educational leadership.* Invited Address, Division A, AERA, Montreal, Quebec, Canada.

Ogawa, R. T. (1994). "The Institutional Sources of Educational Reform: The Case of School-Based Management." *American Educational Research Journal,* 31(3):519–548.

Postman, N. (1993). *Technopoly: The surrender of technology to culture.* New York: Vintage Books.

Price, W. J., and Achilles, C. M. (2000). "Doctor, lawyer, military chief: Superintendents for the new millennium?" *The AASA Professor,* 23(2): 28–34.

Quint, B. (2003). "ERIC Continues but Without Clearinghouses." *Information Today.* Available online: http://www.infotoday.com/newsbreaks/nb030421-1.shtml

Schlechty, P. (1997). *Inventing better schools: An action plan for educational reform.* San Francisco, CA: Jossey-Bass, Inc.

Sergiovanni, T. (1996). *Leadership for the schoolhouse.* San Francisco, CA: Jossey-Bass, Inc.

Sergiovanni, T. (1999). *Building community in schools.* San Francisco, CA: Jossey-Bass, Inc.

Shepard, L. A., and Smith, M. L. (1989). *Flunking grades: Research and policies on retention.* London: Falmer Press.

Shipman, N., and Murphy, J. (1996). *ISLLC: Standards for school leaders.* Adopted by Full Consortium. Washington, DC: Council of Chief State School Officers of CCSSO.

VanMeter, E., and Murphy, J. (1997). *Using ISLLC standards to strengthen preparation programs in school administration.* Washington, DC: Council of Chief State School Officers.

Conclusion

As faculty, staff, students, alumni, and the rest of the world grow more accustomed to using technology in their everyday lives, demands for technological solutions on college campuses will continue to increase rapidly. I anticipate that the pace of technological change on college campuses will outpace that of society in general; after all, we are preparing students for a society that will continue to change through the use of technology.

The cases profiled in this book reflect schools that have taken risks to provide better services to their communities. These schools are to be commended for using technology in creative or nontraditional ways to further the mission of their institutions.

About the Contributors and Project Leaders

Kari Branjord

Kari Branjord is the director of Web Development at the University of Minnesota. Email: branj002@umn.edu.

Francisco (Frank) Chang

Francisco (Frank) Chang is the system analyst and technical liaison for the Office of Academic Records & Registrar at University of Southern California (USC). He was responsible for testing the various alpha and beta versions of the system prior to deployment and writing, designing, and encoding the online user instructions as well as the Flash-enhanced tutorial. Frank has a BS in Kinesiology and an MCSE license. E-mail: fjc@usc.edu

John W. Collins, Jr.

Dr. John W. Collins, Jr., Ed.D. has over a quarter-century of experience between the United States Army and several educational institutions. Currently he serves on the faculty at Seton Hall University (NJ) in the College of Education and Human Services with the Department of Education Leadership, Management and Policy. His teaching and research interests are adult education, leadership, administration, educational technology and distance learning. E-mail: collinjo@shu.edu

Terry Corwin

Dr. Terry Corwin has served as the Director of Instructional Technology at Valley City State University (ND) for the past seven years. She facilitates the student electronic portfolio process on the campus and assists with the campuswide notebook computer initiative. She was a co-coordinator for the NCA self-study in 2001 and has been a successful grant writer and director for the past two years. Previously she was a faculty member in the division of Health and Physical Education at VCSU. Terry received her B.A. in health & physical education from Gustavus Adolphus College, an M.S. in physical education from Minnesota State University at Moorhead, and a Ph.D. in Instructional Technology from Iowa State University. E-mail: terry_corwin@mail.vcsu.nodak.edu

Rebecca Frost Davis

Rebecca Frost Davis is the Assistant Director for Instructional Technology at the Associated Colleges of the South Technology Center (TX), where she works with classicists, IT staff, software engineering faculty and interns, as well as other groups interested in inter-institutional collaboration. Rebecca received her Ph.D. in Classical Studies from the University of Pennsylvania, and has been a faculty member at Southwest Missouri State University, Rhodes College, Denison University, and the University of the South. E-mail: rdavis@colleges.org

Dennis V. Day

Dennis V. Day has been with Johnson County Community College (KS) since 1984 and is the Dean of Student Services. Throughout his tenure he has been an advocate of innovative student systems and proponent of the recently built Student Success Center, which provides students with a one stop for admissions, advisement, assessment, career planning, enrollment, and financial aid. Using Web-based services and personalized attention, students are encouraged to engage in self-service processes where appropriate. With a doctorate in higher education from the University of Kansas, Dr. Day has been in education for 27 years. E-mail: dday@jccc.net

Fred Dear

Fred Dear has been employed in the Registrars' profession at University of Southern California (USC) since 1966 and received his MS in Education from the university in 1969. He was directly involved in the design and implementation of the first online integrated registration system in 1980; composed most of the voicecom script for the implementation of the TouchTone registration system in 1988; and in 2001 participated in the design and release of the new Web-based registration system. E-mail: dear@usc.edu

Michael (M. P.) Evans

Dr. Michael Evans is a lecturer at the University of Reading (UK). His interests include Web dynamics, Web technologies, and cultural information flow. E-mail: M.Evans@computer.org

Mary Helen Fagan

Dr. Mary Helen Fagan is an Assistant Professor of Information Systems in the College of Business and Technology at the University of Texas at Tyler. Dr. Fagan has worked as a managerial consultant for Andersen Consulting (now Accenture) and as Manager of User Services in the Academic Computing Services Department at the University of Texas at Arlington. E-mail: mfagan@mail.uttyl.edu

A. C. M. Fong

A.C.M. Fong is an Assistant Professor in Computer Engineering at Nanyang Technological University (Singapore). His research interests include various aspects of Internet and multimedia technologies, and communications. He graduated from Imperial College, London and University of Auckland. He is a member of IEEE and IEE, and is a Chartered Engineer registered in the UK. E-mail: acmfong@pmail.ntu.edu.sg.

Steven (S. M.) Furnell

Dr. Steven Furnell is currently a Reader at the University of Plymouth (UK). His interests include IT security, Internet and Web technologies, and information society issues. E-mail: sfurnell@network-research-group.org

Jane Gao

Jane Gao has over 14 years of software development experience, specifically in software analyzing and designing. Jane holds a bachelor's degree in Computer Science. Jane is leading many campuswide Web application projects at University of California (UC), Irvine. Jane has been with UC for 10 years. E-mail: jane@uci.edu

Mollie Gore

Mollie Gore is a staff writer for University Relations at Charleston Southern University. E-mail: mgore@csuniv.edu

Nichole Howa Greenwood

Nichole Howa Greenwood is a Telecommunications Coordinator at Westminster College in Salt Lake City, Utah.

Jeff Guan

Jeff Guan is Associate Professor of Computer Information Systems at the University of Louisville. He teaches, writes, and consults on database systems, business intelligence technologies, and e-commerce technologies. He has extensive data warehousing consulting experience with organizations of all sizes, both in the private and public sectors. His current research interests pertain to the organizational and strategic issues in establishing information value chain in higher education. E-mail: jeff.guan@louisville.edu

Thomas Hauck

Thomas Hauck has been employed at University of Southern California (USC) since 1995 and helped design the online student service OASIS (Online Academic Student Information System). His primary involvement is back end and infrastructure technology. He initially started the design and prototype implementation of the Web registration project and later took the lead of a group of four programmers. Thomas has an MS in Electrical Engineering Control Systems and an MS in Computer Networks. He is currently implementing Global Directory Services for the university. E-mail: hauck@usc.edu

Carole A. Hayes

Carole Hayes is the Coordinator for External Relations in the Office for Distributed and Distance Learning at Florida State University. She has worked in continuing education and distance learning for the past 10 years. She came to FSU in August 1998 and was instrumental in the design, development, and implementation of student support services for online learners. E-mail: CHayes@oddl.fsu.edu

S. C. Hui

S. C. Hui is an Associate Professor in the School of Computer Engineering at Nanyang Technological University (Singapore). His current research interests include data mining, Internet technology, and multimedia systems. He received his B.Sc. degree in Mathematics in 1983 and a D. Phil. degree in Computer Science in 1987 from the University of Sussex, UK. He worked in IBM China/Hong Kong Corporation as a system engineer from 1987 to 1990. E-mail: asschui@ntu.edu.sg

Eric Jansson

Eric Jansson is the Assistant Director for Systems and Development at the Associated Colleges of the South Technology Center (TX). Eric specializes in software design and requirements analysis for learning management and educational content management systems. He has been developing software for secondary and university-level institutions for the past 6 years in both the commercial and public spheres. Eric attended Cornell University and has a Masters degree in English from the University of Texas at Austin. He studied Computer Science at UT Austin. E-mail: ejansson@colleges.org

Les Lloyd

Les is associate vice-president for Information Technology at Rollins College in Winter Park, Florida. In that role, Les is responsible for all areas of technology including academic and administrative computing, networking and systems, desktop and laptop repair as well as instructional technology. Les has worked in higher education technology administration for over 20 years and has published several books on the various areas of higher education technology. E-mail: llloyd@rollins.edu

Del Lovitt

Del Lovitt, Senior Data Integration Analyst at Johnson County Community College (KS), leads implementation teams of projects to completion, and consults on services to Student Services staff in association with the business process as it interfaces with the administrative computing system. In her current position, her primary objective is to understand and help implement institutional visions. Del has a Bachelor of Science degree from Fort Hays State University. E-mail: dlovitt@jccc.net.

Eunice M. Merideth

Dr. Eunice M. Merideth is the Associate Dean and a Professor in the Drake University (IA) School of Education. She has designed and taught courses with and about technology for 16 years at the university level and worked with technology integration at all levels of education. She has also been an Academic Computing Fellow with Drake University, a position that supported Web-assisted and Web-based instruction by providing curriculum and Web design as well as professional development for faculty across the university. Besides support activities, Dr. Merideth has led an interdisciplinary team of professors in designing and implementing an all-university concentration for Studies in Information Technology. E-mail: eunice.merideth @drake.edu

Chris Muñoz

Chris Muñoz, former Vice President for Enrollment Management at the University of Dayton, has 30 years of professional experience in enrollment management including student recruitment, admission, financial aid and the office of the registrar. Muñoz has held positions at California Lutheran University, Humboldt State University, the University of Oregon and the University of California, Irvine. Muñoz, who holds a bachelor's degree in theater arts from California State University, Fullerton and a master's degree in counseling psychology from the University of Oregon, is now Vice Provost for Enrollment Management at Case Western Reserve University. E-mail: chris. munoz@notes.udayton.edu

William Nunez

William Nunez is Associate Director for Planning and Budget at the University of Louisville. He is completing a doctorate in educational administration in postsecondary education at the University of Louisville. He has published in higher education journals on the role of information systems in institutional planning and strategic development. E-mail: wjnunez@louisville.edu

Elaine Peters

Elaine Peters' background includes 15 years of Human Resources industry experience, specifically specializing in the employment and staffing arena and a bachelor's degree in Human Resources Management. Elaine manages the Employment function for the University of California (UC) Irvine Campus. E-mail: epeters@ uci.edu

Suzanne Petrusch

After six years as the Director of Enrollment Management Operations at the University of Dayton, Suzanne Petrusch was named the Director of Marketing for Enrollment Management effective July 1, 2001. She coordinates and implements the marketing and communications plans for the enrollment management division, integrating various media and new technologies. She holds a Bachelor of Science in business administration from Trinity University and a Master of Science in education from the University of Dayton. Together with Chris Muñoz, she is a requested speaker at national conferences and delights in sharing information about the use of technology as a critical component of the University of Dayton's enrollment management and positioning strategies. E-mail: spetrusch@ udayton.edu

Paul Reynolds

Paul Reynolds, Ph.D., is a professor at the University of Plymouth (UK).

Marcus Robinson

Marcus Robinson began his association with the University of Dayton as a political science student in 1995, and was hired as a full-time staff member in 1998. He collaborates with Skill, Muñoz, Petrusch, and other key players to create ways in which the university will use Internet technology to sustain a competitive advantage. In managing the Internet Development Division, Robinson oversees the planning and development of innovative Web applications that enhance learning and support personal development. E-mail: marcus.robinson@ notes.udayton.edu

Stephan Ross

Stephan Ross is a Computer Support Manager and Webmaster in the Information and Technology Department at Westminster College in Salt Lake City, Utah.

Nancy Sinsabaugh

Nancy Sinsabaugh has been the interim director of the Office of Student Finance and interim director of the Office of Scholarships and Financial Aid at the University of Minnesota since 1999. She was the architect of "paperless financial aid" at the university and directed financial aid, student billing, and student loan operations at the university's four campuses.

Before joining the University of Minnesota, she was a student services consultant in Minnesota for two years, consulting higher education institutions on student services. Nancy also served as the director of student financial services at Harvard University from 1985 to 1993. E-mail: nsins@earthlink.net

Peggy E. Steinbronn

Peggy E. Steinbronn, Ed.S., is the Instructional Technology Specialist at Drake University (IA). She holds an Education Specialist degree in Curriculum Design with a Technology concentration. She has been an educator in the K-12 school system and at the university level. In her support role at Drake, she collaborates with faculty individually and assists them in honing their technology skills and online instructional strategies by leading faculty development workshops in the pedagogy of online instruction and design. She also provides assistance and support for online students and is the administrator of Drake's online courseware. E-mail: peggy.steinbronn@drake.edu

Ronnie Swanner

Ronnie Swanner is the Director of Instructional Media Services at Trinity University in San Antonio, Texas. He holds a BS degree in biology from Baylor University and an MA degree in Instructional Technology from Texas A&M University. He is a graduate of the Audiovisual Institute for Effective Communications, Indiana University and has certificates in Systems and Facility Design from the International Communications Academy in Washington D.C. He has provided consultant services to the U.S. Navel Academy, Annapolis, Maryland, School of Aerospace Medicine, U.S. Air Force, Brooks Air Force Base, San Antonio, Texas, The University of Texas at San Antonio, Texas, and the Academy of Health Sciences, U.S. Army, Fort Sam Houston, Texas. E-mail: RSwanner@Trinity.edu

Pat Ullmann

Pat Ullmann is the Production Manager in the department of Instructional Media Services at Trinity University in San Antonio, Texas. She holds a BA degree in geology from Trinity, where she was a Presidential Scholar. Her current management responsibilities include Trinity's Multimedia Development Center computer lab, the campus closed-circuit television information channel, and the campus video streaming system. E-mail: PUllmann@Trinity.edu

John F. Welsh

John F. Welsh is Associate University Provost and Associate Professor of Education at the University of Louisville. His administrative duties encompass assessment, institutional effectiveness, distance education, and faculty development. He teaches courses in higher education organization and higher education finance. His current research interests pertain to the role of assessment and information systems in organizational change in higher education. E-mail: john.welsh@louisville.edu

Index

Page numbers in *italics* are used to indicate that the information is located in tables or figures.

D

G

H

I

J

K

L

M

N

O

P

T

U

X

Y